SKI
WHISTLE

by Brian Finestone & Kevin Hodder

Aerial photography courtesy Damian Cromwell, Scott Flavelle and the authors. All uncredited photographs by the authors.

Front cover photo of the Blackcomb Glacier by Scott Flavelle.

Research and text:
Knee Deep Productions
Box 1456 Whistler, B.C. V0N 1B0
www.whistlerguidebooks.com

Printed and bound in Canada at Kromar Printing.

Layout, design and distribution:
Quickdraw Publications
Box 1786   Squamish, B.C.   V0N 3G0
Fax: (604) 892-9281
Web: www.quickdrawpublications.com

Title page and back cover photographs by Insight Photography.

Table of Contents

Read this before you use this book!

Warning: Skiing and snowboarding are sports with inherent risks. Participating in these sports may result in injury or death.

This guidebook is intended for skiers and snowboarders with a minimum of intermediate ability and experience. The terrain described within can be dangerous and requires a high level of fitness and attention to negotiate.

This guidebook is a compilation of information from several sources. As a result the authors cannot confirm the accuracy of any specific detail. Difficulty ratings are subjective and may vary depending on your own personal experience and the conditions on the mountain. There may be misinformation in regards to run description, condition, or difficulty.

This guidebook does not give the user the right to access any terrain described within. The Ski Patrol may limit access to any part of the mountain at any time. It is your responsibility to adhere to all closures.

This guidebook is not a substitute for experience and proper judgment. The authors, publisher and distributors of this book do not recognize any liability for injury or damage caused to, or by skiers and snowboarders, third parties or property arising from such persons seeking reliance on this guidebook as an assurance of their own safety. Your use of this book indicates your assumption of the risk that it may contain errors and is an acknowledgment of your own sole responsibility for your safety.

Matt Elliot catches *large air* by Tiger's Terrace on Whistler Mountain. Photo: Damian Cromwell

The inspiration for this book came from the recognition that Whistler and Blackcomb are blessed with over 11,000 skiable acres, four glaciers, over 20 alpine bowls and 33 lifts. These are two huge mountains and finding your way around can be very confusing (even with careful consultation of the trail map). Without someone showing you around it can take the better part of a season just to figure out what your favorite runs are and how to access them. In short, anyone coming for a week-long vacation has to learn pretty fast! This book is an attempt to

Blackcomb

remedy this issue by presenting detailed information of the ski area in a user-friendly format.

As dedicated rock-climbers, the authors have used guidebooks that would allow them to show up at a distant climbing area and enjoy the best routes almost immediately. The intention of this book is to bring a format long used by authors of climbing guidebooks to the ski area.

Over 11,000 acres of skiable terrain!

Whistler

How To Use This Book

Congratulations! You have purchased the ultimate reference for intermediate skiers and snowboarders wishing to maximize their experience at Whistler Blackcomb. Each chapter within this book gives an overview of the terrain that is accessed by a specific chairlift. Run and access information is presented in a number of ways including aerial photographs, symbols and text. The aerial photographs are superimposed with labels and markings and become an excellent tool for choosing what area you want to explore next. The symbols are used to provide a significant amount of information at a glance.

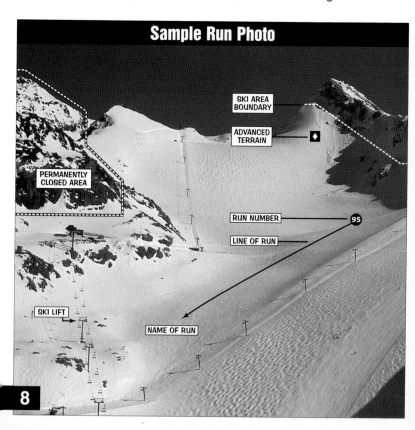

Sample Run Photo

SKI AREA BOUNDARY

ADVANCED TERRAIN

PERMANENTLY CLOSED AREA

RUN NUMBER — 95

LINE OF RUN

SKI LIFT

NAME OF RUN

Please refer to the key below to familiarize yourself with the symbol definitions. The written text is intended to provide any further information that cannot be directly presented through photograph or symbol.

This book is designed to be used in conjunction with the mountain trail map. Trail maps are available free of charge throughout the resort and for viewing at www.whistlerblackcomb.com/maps/. Keep both the map and this book handy while riding on the mountain. Both are pocket size for a reason!

Symbols

Symbol	Definition	Symbol	Definition	Symbol	Definition
	The 'tick' box		Platter Lift		Olympic venue
	Novice run		Handle Tow		Designated slow zone
	Novice plus run		Gondola		Great views
	Intermediate run		T-Bar		Must-hike-up-to access
	Intermediate plus run		Triple chairlift		Run is commonly deserted
	Expert run		Quad chairlift		Flat areas - some poling required
	Average run		Chairlift is down-load capable		A long, thigh-burning run
	Good run		Powder common on this slope		Often crowded
	Excellent run		Moguls common on this slope		Watch for skidoos
	Teaching area		Regularly groomed		Narrow run
	Snow park for kids		Treed		Falling off a cliff hazard
	Terrain park		Great cruising run		Avalanche debris

9

Anleitung Zu Diesem Buch

Herzlichen Glückwunsch! Sie haben das ultimative Handbuch für fortgeschrittene Ski- und Snowboardanfänger erworben, welche den Wunsch haben Ihre Erfahrungen in Whistler Blackcomb zu maximieren. Jedes Kapitel in diesem Buch gibt einen Überblick über das Gelände, zugänglich mit einem bestimmten Sessellift. Pisten- und Zugangsinformationen sind dargestellt auf verschiedene Arten wie Luftaufnahmen, Symbole und Texte. Die Luftaufnahmen sind markiert mit Labels und Kennzeichnungen und sind ein ausgezeichnetes Hilfsmittel, um die Gegend auszuwählen, welche Sie als nächstes erkunden wollen. Die Symbole werden eingesetzt, um eine bedeutende Anzahl Informationen auf einen Blick zu haben.

Wir verweisen auf den folgenden Schlüssel, um sich mit den Symboldefinitionen vertraut zu machen. Mit dem Text wird beabsichtigt, weitere Informationen zu geben, welche nicht direkt dargestellt sind auf Photos oder durch Symbole.

Dieses Buch ist konzipiert worden, um es zusammen mit der Skigebietskarte zu benützen. Skigebietskarten sind gratis erhältlich überall im Resort und zur Ansicht unter www.whistlerblackcomb.com/maps. Halten Sie beides, Karte und Buch, griffbereit bei Ihren Abfahrten am Berg. Schliesslich sind beide Taschenformat aus einem Grund!

Symbole

Symbol	Bedeutung	Symbol	Bedeutung	Symbol	Bedeutung
☐	Das 'erledigt' Kästchen	🏃	Tellerlift		Olympischer Austragungsort
●	Anfängerpiste		Schlepplift		Gekennzeichnete Langsamzone
⊕	Anfänger'plus'-Piste		Gondelbahn	◎	Grossartige Aussicht
☐	Mittelschwere Piste		Bügellift		Zugang muss erklommen werden
⊞	Mittelschwer'plus'-Piste		Dreiersessel		Meist ausgestorbene Piste
◆	Expertenpiste		Vierersessel		Flaches Gebiet, verlangt Stockeinsatz
❶	Durchschnittliche Piste		Sessellift mit Talfahrtmöglichkeit		Eine lange, oberschenkelbrennende Abfahrt
❷	Schöne Piste	POW	Mit Pulverschnee darf gerechnet werden		Oft überfüllt
❸	Ausgezeichnete Piste		Mit Buckel darf gerechnet werden		Vorsicht Schneemobils
🍎	Skischulgebiet	▨	Regelmässig gepistet	N	Enge Piste
	Schneepark für Kinder	🌲	Bewaldet		Absturzgefahr über Felsen
Ⓣ	Fun park		'Carving-Piste'		Lawinenkegel

11

本書の活用法

　ウィスラー・ブラッコムへようこそ！　本書は初級者から中～上級者までのスキーヤー・スノーボーダーの方たちを対象にまとめられたゲレンデガイドです。広大な２つのスキー場を効率よく楽しんでいただくための情報が満載されています。各章は、各チェアリフトからアクセスできるコースごとに分けて説明してあります。また、写真にはシンボルマークを挿入し、一見してコースの情報を得られるように工夫いたしました。

コース案内表示例

スキー場境界線

エキスパートコース ◆

立ち入り禁止区域

コース番号 95

滑走ライン

チェアリフト

コース名

　本書はリゾート内の至るところで手に入れることができる無料のゲレンデマップ（Trail Map）と合わせてご覧頂くことを前提に編集されています。ゲレンデマップは、ホテルのフロント、スキー場内のレストランやリフト・ゴンドラ乗場などに置かれています。またインターネットからも閲覧することができます。（www.whistlerblackcomb.com/maps/）スキー場に向かわれる際は、ゲレンデマップと併せて本書を携帯されるようお勧めいたします。

シンボルマーク

滑ったらここをチェック	ロープトゥ	オリンピック競技予定コース
初級者コース	ハンドルトゥ	スピード規制エリア
初級者～中級者コース	ゴンドラ	ビューポイント
中級者コース	Tバーリフト	ハイクアップ
中級者～上級者コース	3人乗りチェアリフト	空いているコース
エキスパートコース	4人乗り高速リフト	平坦部
お勧め度（中）	下り線利用可能なチェアリフト	ロングコース
お勧め度（高）	非圧雪エリア	混雑するコース
お勧め度（最高）	コブ斜面	スノーモービルに注意
レッスン専用エリア	圧雪バーン	細くて狭いコース
子供用パーク	立木あり	崖に注意
パーク	クルージング向き	雪崩跡に注意

13

Cómo Usar Esta Guía

Felicitaciones, Usted ha adquirido el mejor libro de referencia para esquiadores y snowbordistas que posean un nivel intermedio, y que desean aprovechar al máximo su experiencia en Whistler Blackcomb.

Cada capítulo del libro brinda un panorama del sector que puede ser visitado con cada uno de los medios de elevación. La información acerca de las pistas y los accesos está presentada de varias maneras, incluyendo fotografías aéreas, símbolos y textos. Las fotografías aéreas llevan superpuestas marcas e indicaciones y se convierten en una excelente herramienta para elegir cuál será la próxima área a explorar. Los símbolos brindan rápidamente una gran cantidad de información.

Por favor, consulte la guía presentada más abajo para familiarizarse con las definiciones de los símbolos. El texto escrito está pensado para proveer toda aquella información que no puede ser dada a través de fotografías o símbolos.

Este libro está diseñado para ser usado en conjunto con un mapa de senderos de la montaña. Estos mapas pueden ser obtenidos sin cargo en varios lugares del complejo y también en www.whistlerblckcomb.com/maps. Le recomendamos que tenga siempre a mano este libro y el mapa cuando esté recorriendo la montaña. ¡Por algo es una edición de bolsillo!

Símbolos

☐	Planilla de verificación	🏂	Estera mecánica		Facilidad olímpica
●	Pista para novicios		Rope tow (manual)		Zona de baja velocidad
⊕	Pista para novicios avanzados		Góndola	📷	Vista panorámica
☐	Pista para esquiadores intermedios		"T bar" o Barra T		Debe caminar para acceder
⊞	Pista para esquiadores intermedios avanzados	👥	Aerosilla triple		Pista normalmente desierta
◆	Pista para expertos	👥	Aerosilla cuádruple		Área plana que requiere ayudarse con los bastones
1	Pista de dificultad media		Aerosilla que permite el descenso		Pista larga que exige mucho esfuerzo
2	Pista buena	POW	Nieve en polvo es común en este sector		Pista normalmente muy concurrida
3	Pista excelente		Es común encontrar "moguls" en este sector		Cuidado con las motos de nieve
🍎	Área de práctica	▨	Pista acondicionada regularmente	N	Pista angosta
	Área infantil	🌲	Pista arbolada		Peligro de desbarrancarse
T	Snow park		Descenso sumamente placentero		Residuos de avalancha

Safety

Your safety is of paramount concern at Whistler Blackcomb. The Ski Patrol and Mountain Safety Team work hard to reduce the risk of accidents at the resort. Reckless skiing and snowboarding are taken very seriously and people who ride in this manner will lose their skiing privileges.

Safety starts with the Alpine Responsibility Code. The code is an internationally recognized safety system and is posted in public areas at all ski resorts. It has also been adopted as law in several states.

The Alpine Responsibility Code

THERE ARE INHERENT RISKS in all snow-based recreational activities that common sense and personal awareness can reduce. These risks include rapid changes in weather and surface conditions, collisions with other people, and natural and artificial hazards such as rocks, trees, stumps, bare spots, lift towers and snowmaking equipment.

Know and observe the code — It's YOUR responsibility. Failure to observe the Alpine Responsibility Code may result in CANCELLATION of your lift ticket by the Ski Patrol or other authorized personnel.

ALPINE
RESPONSIBILITY CODE

THERE ARE ELEMENTS OF RISK THAT COMMON SENSE AND PERSONAL AWARENESS CAN HELP REDUCE. REGARDLESS OF HOW YOU DECIDE TO USE THE SLOPES, ALWAYS SHOW COURTESY TO OTHERS. PLEASE ADHERE TO THE CODE LISTED BELOW AND SHARE WITH OTHERS THE RESPONSIBILITY FOR A SAFE OUTDOOR EXPERIENCE.

1 *Always stay in control. You must be able to stop, or avoid other people or objects.*

2 *People ahead of you have the right-of-way. It is your responsibility to avoid them.*

3 *Do not stop where you obstruct a trail or are not visible from above.*

4 *Before starting downhill or merging onto a trail, look uphill and yield to others.*

5 *If you are involved in or witness a collision or accident, you must remain at the scene and identify yourself to the Ski Patrol.*

6 *Always use proper devices to help prevent runaway equipment.*

7 *Observe and obey all posted signs and warnings.*

8 *Keep off closed trails and closed areas.*

9 *You must not use lifts or terrain if your ability is impaired through use of alcohol or drugs.*

10 *You must have sufficient physical dexterity, ability and knowledge to safely load, ride and unload lifts. If in doubt, ask the lift attendant.*

Know the Code - Be Safety Conscious
It is Your Responsibility

Additional Safety Tips

Please consider the following safety recommendations:

- ☐ The runs at Whistler Blackcomb can be extremely busy. Like driving your car in traffic, it is important to ski or snowboard defensively, particularly on busy days. Always be aware of your surroundings. Collisions between skiers are alarmingly common.

- ☐ Avoid stopping in the middle of the run and <u>never</u> stop in places where other riders can't see you.

- ☐ Think about the potential speeds involved in skiing and snowboarding. A helmet can offer a significant safety margin. Wear one!

- ☐ Accidents often happen when you're tired. Consider riding the lift back down to the valley if your legs are feeling tired at the end of your day. "Downloading" avoids the high traffic of the ski-out, allows for great panoramic sight seeing and saves your legs so you can have a great day tomorrow. Most chairs allow for downloading.

- ☐ Avoid skiing alone. Not only is it more fun to ride with a friend, but it provides for someone to be there in case of an accident.

Helmets are a safety necessity.

What to do if you or someone in your group is injured:

- First and foremost cross a pair of skis uphill of the injured skier. This will alert skiers above that someone is lying down on the snow and will signal to everyone that the Ski Patrol is required.

- If the injured person is hidden from the view of skiers above, cross a pair of skis on top of the mound or feature that is hiding the skier. The other pair of skis should stay crossed just above the patient.

- Make sure the Ski Patrol have been alerted to the fact that you need assistance. Wave down a skier and have him or her tell the operator at the bottom of the nearest lift that you need assistance. Make sure that the responding skier can tell the operator what run you are on, approximately where on the run you are (i.e. halfway down, near lift tower 17, etc.) and what the injury is. If you have a cell phone, call the patrol dispatch at (604) 935-5555.

Cross your skis above the injured skier.

Safety Strategies For Skiing With Children

Please consider the following safety recommendations:

- ☐ Small children must get on the chair in the position closest to the lift operator. This way, the operator can assist the child onto the chair.

- ☐ Lower the safety bar as soon as you get on the chairlift.

- ☐ Hang on to little skiers on the chair at all times.

- ☐ Do not let children (on anyone for that matter) lean on the door of the Gondolas.

- ☐ Arrange a place to meet in case you get separated from your child.

- ☐ Provide children with a card that lists the parents' name, phone number and hotel.

- ☐ Ensure that your children can recognize a member of the Ski Patrol and that they know they can always go to them if they are lost or require assistance.

- ☐ Have your child carry a whistle. They may be able to signal for help more effectively than by voice.

- ☐ Ski in the Beginner Zones and Family Zones where the speed of all skiers is restricted.

- ☐ Enjoy yourself! Visit the Tree Fort on Whistler and the Magic Castle on Blackcomb.

Tree Wells: More people are killed in coastal snow regions by tree wells than by avalanches!

A tree well is a phenomenon unique to big mountains with deep snow packs. A tree well forms when snow falling on evergreens accumulates between the trees but not around the tree trunk. As the snow is shed from the branches above it falls away from the tree creating a moat around the base of the trunk. As the snow gets deeper so does the tree well.

The danger of the tree well exists when a person falls over in the snow and ends up with their body upside down in the tree well. As the person struggles to get out, the hole fills with snow, potentially burying the victim. People have died of suffocation in the wells of both large trees and small saplings. The hazard exists anywhere on the mountain once the snowpack exceeds one meter (3.5 feet) in depth.

Whistler Blackcomb recognizes that children like the challenge of skiing and snowboarding narrow trails through the trees and have created unique areas where this is possible and the tree well hazard is reduced. Refer to the family section for specific information on these areas.

Dropping the knee in the trees.

Trail Designations ⬤ ⊕ ▢ ⊞ ◆

All ski runs are not created equal! Many people find the Blue runs at Whistler to be as hard as the Black Diamond runs at other ski areas. So, how do they classify the runs at Whistler Blackcomb? Trails are given a difficulty rating based on an evaluation of the slope's width, average gradient, and the steepest 30 meters of pitch. A simple rating of Green, Blue or Black Diamond does not do the variety of terrain at Whistler Blackcomb justice, therefore, we have added Green Plus and Blue Plus to this guide to fill in the gaps between ratings. Remember, with the increase in difficulty comes an increase in the risk of longer and more hazardous falls!

Signs

The following is the interpretation of some of the signage at Whistler Blackcomb and the consequences of skiing beyond them.

Ski Area Boundary

This sign indicates the border of Whistler Blackcomb's patrolled area. Skiing or riding outside the area is done at your own risk. It is your responsibility to have the adequate knowledge to travel safely in avalanche terrain and to carry the essential personal-safety gear. People who require rescue from the backcountry can and will be charged for their rescue

In early season, Ski Area Boundary signs often exist within the ski area. These boundaries denote parts of the hill that are not yet ready to open. As a result, there are no hazard markings, no patrols, and no sweep of these areas at the end of the day.

Permanently Closed

These signs indicate areas of the mountain that are NEVER open. These are areas within the ski area that are determined to be unsuitable for skiing. The danger of entering these areas often extends beyond the risk to the offending skier or rider, because their actions threaten skiers on runs below. Passes will be revoked from anyone who disobeys these signs.

Closed / Avalanche Hazard

Avalanche Closure signs are used to temporarily close areas within the ski area. Avalanche Closures keep guests out of harm's way during active avalanche control (explosives!) or when the hazard grows too high and control is not possible. Passes will be revoked from anyone who disobeys these signs.

Closed

Runs are closed for a variety of reasons. These reasons may include: thin snow cover, ditches or holes, fallen trees, races or other events are taking place, snowmaking or other machinery is operating, etc. Passes will be revoked from anyone who disobeys these signs.

Signs

Marginal Skiing

Marginal Skiing signs are used to mark runs that have limited snow cover but are still determined "skiable" by the Patrol. These runs may have exposed rocks, grass and dirt. Incurring damage to your skis or snowboard on these runs is possible. It is best to avoid these runs, or at the very least, ski or ride with extreme caution. The Ski Patrol will mark <u>some</u> hazards on these runs and perform a sweep at the end of the ski day.

Unmarked Rocks and Obstacles

This warning is posted at the top of a chairlift to warn skiers that many natural hazards off the groomed trails are not marked. These hazards can damage skis and snowboards or cause injury to riders. Ski and snowboard with caution.

Experts Only

This sign indicates that the terrain beyond is not suitable for intermediate or beginner skiers, even if Blue and Green runs exist. This sign is posted at the base of a chairlift in the event that weather has made the runs more difficult and/or grooming is nonexistent. Poor visibility will also result in this type of warning.

At the bottom of the Peak Chair on Whistler Mountain, a flashing orange light will be activated when only advanced and expert conditions can be accessed by the lift.

Useful Phone Numbers

WHISTLER BLACKCOMB SNOW PHONE

(604) 932 4211 - WHISTLER

(604) 687 7507 - VANCOUVER

ON-MOUNTAIN EMERGENCY

(604) 935 5555

AFTER-HOURS EMERGENCY

(604) 905 5484 - MISSING PERSONS

Website

This site contains excellent information on weather, snow conditions, avalanche hazard, road conditions, events, live web cams, etc.

www.whistlerblackcomb.com

Operating Hours

DATE	OPENING	CLOSING
NOV - JAN 28	8:30 AM	3:00 PM
JAN 29 - FEB 27	8:30 AM	3:30 PM
FEB 28 - APR 17	8:30 AM	4:00 PM
APR 18 - JUN 5	9:00 AM	4:00 PM

SnowCovers

www.snowcovers.com

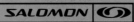 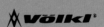

Photo: Toshi Kawano

THE SKY'S THE LIMIT.

At Whistler Blackcomb, we make it easy to keep everyone happy. Free guided mountain tours, terrain for all abilities, family fun at the new Tube Park and our Ski & Snowboard School provide choice and variety for everybody. There may not be enough hours in the day to do it all, but of course, there's always tomorrow.

Visit any Guest Relations counter or call **604.932.3434** or **1.800.766.0449**.

40 25

ANNIVERSARIES

For the latest information on mountain conditions call the Snowphone at **604.932.4211** or visit **whistlerblackcomb.com**

WHISTLER. ALWAYS REAL.

Whistler Blackcomb is proud to be a venue for the 2010 Olympic and Paralympic Winter Games.

INTRAWEST

WHISTLER BLACKCOMB

From Vancouver International Airport

If you are arriving at Vancouver International Airport (www.yvr.ca), one of the best ways to get to Whistler is by shuttle bus. The shuttle allows you to defer the potentially harrowing experience of driving Highway 99 in winter conditions to a professional driver. Also, once in Whistler, you will likely not need a vehicle. This is because the vast majority of accommodation is within walking (or skiing!) distance from the lifts, shopping and restaurants. Perimeter Whistler Express offers 11 departures per day to and from Whistler. It costs about $65 CAN each way. Reservations are recommended ((877) 317-7788, www.perimeterbus.com/express.html). More-exclusive options such as limousines and helicopter transfers are also available.

If you do choose to drive, the standard array of car rental outlets exists at the arrivals level of the airport.

Driving to Whistler

The main route to Whistler rambles through the downtown core of Vancouver before reaching the winding Sea to Sky Highway (Highway 99 north of Horseshoe Bay). The drive is one of the most scenic in North America and has adequate signage to keep you on route. Highway 99 is not, however, without its hazards. Poor weather and impatient motorists cause accidents each year, and it is essential to drive defensively. Good winter-rated tires are required during the season, and in the worst weather, chains become mandatory.

Map of Western Canada and USA

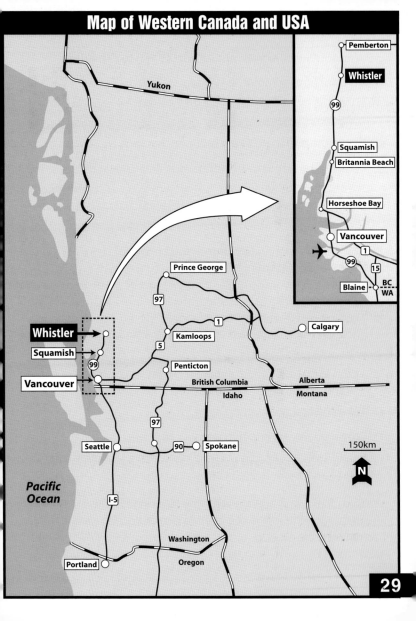

Getting To And From Whistler

▭⟶ **Vancouver International Airport (YVR) to Whistler**

Travel Time: approximately 2 ¼ hours

Distance: 135 kilometers or 85 miles

- ☐ Leave the airport on Grant McConachie Way.

- ☐ Look for the Highway 99 north signs and follow them over the Arthur Lang Bridge onto Granville Street.

- ☐ Follow Granville Street north until you get on the Granville Street Bridge.

- ☐ Shift into the right-hand lane on the bridge and take the Seymour Street exit.

- ☐ Follow Seymour Street north to Georgia Street.

- ☐ Turn left onto Georgia Street and follow it through downtown and over the spectacular Lions Gate Bridge.

- ☐ Exit the bridge on the Marine Drive West turnoff.

- ☐ Merge to the far-right lane, once on Marine Drive.

- ☐ Take the first right, onto Taylor Way.

- ☐ Travel up the hill and turn left onto Highway 1.

- ☐ Follow Highway 1 until Exit 2, near the Horseshoe Bay ferry terminal.

- ☐ Take Exit 2 and stay on Highway 99 north to Whistler. You will go through the towns of Britannia Beach and Squamish before reaching the resort.

⟹ **Downtown Vancouver to Whistler**

Travel Time: approximately 2 hours

Distance: 120 kilometers or 75 miles

- ☐ Take Georgia Street north toward Stanley Park and follow it over Lions Gate Bridge.

- ☐ Exit the bridge on the Marine Drive West turnoff.

- ☐ Merge to the far-right lane, once on Marine Drive.

- ☐ Take the first right, onto Taylor Way.

- ☐ Travel up the hill and turn left onto Highway 1.

- ☐ Follow Highway 1 until Exit 2, near the Horseshoe Bay ferry terminal.

- ☐ Take Exit 2 and stay on Highway 99 north to Whistler. You will go through the towns of Britannia Beach and Squamish before reaching the resort.

The stunning Mount Garibaldi, just north of Squamish.

Getting To And From Whistler

▭▷ **Seattle to Whistler**

Travel Time: approximately 5 hours

Distance: 340 kilometers or 210 miles

- ☐ Follow I-5 north for approximately 160 kilometers or 100 miles to the Canada-U.S. border.

- ☐ Once across the border, I-5 becomes Highway 99. Follow Highway 99 north for approximately 50 kilometers or 30 miles and cross the Oak Street Bridge.

- ☐ Turn left onto West 41st Avenue.

- ☐ Turn right onto Granville Street.

- ☐ Follow Granville Street north until you get on the Granville Street Bridge.

- ☐ Shift into the right-hand lane on the bridge and take the Seymour Street exit.

- ☐ Follow Seymour Street north to Georgia Street.

- ☐ Turn left onto Georgia Street and follow it through downtown and over the spectacular Lions Gate Bridge.

- ☐ Exit the bridge on the Marine Drive West turnoff.

- ☐ Merge to the far-right lane, once on Marine Drive.

- ☐ Take the first right, onto Taylor Way.

- ☐ Travel up the hill and turn left onto Highway 1.

- ☐ Follow Highway 1 until Exit 2, near the Horseshoe Bay ferry terminal.

- ☐ Take Exit 2 and stay on Highway 99 north to Whistler. You will go through the towns of Britannia Beach and Squamish before reaching the resort.

Arriving in Whistler:

If you are driving to Whistler, you should prearrange detailed directions to help you find your hotel within the often-confusing village. If you get stuck, you can go to one of several tourist-information centers. One of the more convenient ones is located at the Gateway Loop. To find it, turn off Highway 99 onto Village Gate Boulevard, take your first right, then stay left. The information center will be on your right.

Renting Skis:

The shape and construction of skis and snowboards has changed dramatically over the past five years. Many people believe this has been the most important phase in ski technology since the introduction of metal edges! If your equipment is older than five years, consider renting some of the modern gear. Even if you are not an expert skier, high-performance equipment will make a big difference. Trust us, you will have a better day on the mountain!

All reputable rental shops provide good-quality skis that are well maintained. Because boots are a very personal item, and nothing is worse than having a pair that doesn't fit, it is recommended that you bring your own, if you have them. The better rental shops are open late (until 9 p.m.), and it is strongly recommended that you arrange your gear the night before your first day on the slopes, so you avoid the mad rush in the morning. A couple of advantages to using Whistler Blackcomb High-Performance Rentals (whistlerblackcomb.com) is that you get a discount if you pre-book online, and free storage at the base of each mountain is included.

Recommendations - Whistler or Blackcomb?

Decisions, decisions...

Whister Mountain

Beginner Terrain:

   □ Olympic Station Area: This area is accessed by riding the Whistler Village Gondola to the first stop. The area has extensive low-angle, Green terrain. It is serviced by the "easy-loading" Olympic Chair and a Magic Carpet.

Low-End Intermediate Terrain:

   □ Emerald Express
   □ Lower Whistler Village Gondola

Advanced Intermediate Terrain:

   □ Franz's Chair (only in operation during peak periods)
   □ Big Red Express
   □ Garbanzo Express
   □ Creekside Gondola

High-End Intermediate Terrain:

   □ T-Bars
   □ Harmony Express Chair
   □ The Peak

Recommendations - Whistler or Blackcomb?

Geographically, Whistler Mountain and Blackcomb Mountain are neighbors. The skiing experience at each mountain is, however, quite different. Generally, Blackcomb provides steeper, more "fall-line" runs suitable for the advanced intermediate. The beginner and lower-intermediate skier is recommended to start on Whistler Mountain.

Below is a progressive list of zones on each mountain that will allow you to plan your day around the terrain most appropriate for your family or group.

Blackcomb Mountain

Beginner Terrain:

- ☐ Magic Chair
- ☐ Catskinner Chair

Low-End Intermediate Terrain:

- ☐ Excelerator Chair
- ☐ Wizard Chair

Advanced Intermediate Terrain:

- ☐ Solar Coaster
- ☐ Jersey Cream
- ☐ 7th Heaven

High-End Intermediate:

- ☐ 7th Heaven
- ☐ T-Bars
- ☐ Crystal

photo: Damian Cromwell

Maximizing Your Enjoyment On The Mountain

The following tips will greatly increase your efficiency and enjoyment:

☐ Before you head up the mountain, call the Snow Phone or refer to whistlerblackcomb.com to find out what the current and forecast weather is. This information will allow you to dress appropriately and plan for the day.

☐ Bring your goggles! There are only a few days each season when you don't need them.

☐ On busy days (weekends, holidays and when there are great conditions) it is important to get up the mountain early to beat the crowds at the valley lifts. Remember, all skiers must funnel through one of two lifts on Blackcomb or one of three lifts on Whistler to get out of the valley. Try and be there within half an hour of the lift openings.

☐ Once you are on the upper mountain, avoid skiing down to the valley on busy mornings so you don't have to rejoin the lift-lines in the valley.

☐ Refer to the light boards, grooming maps and grooming signs. These postings tell you what lifts are open, how busy each lift is and which runs were groomed the night before. It is important to note that some Blue runs can become Black runs if they are not groomed. This fact makes it crucial to inform yourself as to where the grooming has occurred.

☐ Avoid the restaurants at midday as they can be extremely busy. Two recommended strategies are, have an early brunch or snack as you ski and have lunch after 1:00 pm. Often the most pleasant time in the big lodge-style restaurants (e.g. Round-house, Rendezvous, Glacier Creek) is at breakfast-time between 9:30 and 10:30.

Fantastic spring cruising. Photo: Insight Photography.

Strategies For Skiing On Foggy Days

A common weather phenomenon in the Coast Mountains is the low-level cloud bank. Of course clouds can occur anywhere in the mountains but on Blackcomb the most common elevation affected by clouds is the band from midway up the Wizard Chair to just below the Rendezvous. At Whistler Mountain the typical cloud zone seems to be from the bottom of Upper Franz's (the bottom of the Garbanzo Express on the village side) to the Roundhouse. Skiing through these clouds has been compared to swimming through milk or being inside a ping-pong ball! Here are some helpful tips for having a good day when low-level clouds exist:

☐ Remember, even in low light, trees will cast some shadow and allow better perception of the slope ahead. If the clouds are affecting visibility above the tree line it is best to avoid these elevations all together. Any Guest Relations desk will have information on visibility in the alpine to help you choose appropriate runs.

☐ If you have to ski through the fog, try riding on the side of the runs beside the trees. As mentioned above, we can rely on the trees to greatly improve our depth perception. The side of the run also has the advantage of being typically less moguled and therefore may be easier to ski when the going gets tough. A final advantage to skiing on the side is that the signs indicating run names, difficulty and direction are typically placed here.

☐ On both Whistler and Blackcomb, the ski patrol marks the easiest route down from the alpine areas with high-visibility plastic discs on poles. These "piste-markers" are in blue, green and orange and can be followed to lower points on the mountain that generally have better visibility.

☐ Finally, even experts have a lot of trouble skiing in poor visibility. Experienced skiers will avoid terrain that they find challenging when they cant see! We recommend everyone follows this advice.

Strategies For Skiing On Rainy Days

Yes, it can rain in Whistler, even in the middle of winter. The good news is that the best rainy day activity in Whistler is…well, skiing! A lot of times when it is raining in the valley it's dumping new snow on the mountain. But even if the freezing level is high you can still have a great day. Look at it this way; the snow will probably be soft and the lift lines small. Here are some ways to make the most of it.

- First the obvious; wear completely waterproof outerwear and make sure your jacket has a hood. Don't even think about wearing anything cotton! Quick-drying synthetic undergarments are essential to stay warm and dry.

- Consider the good old garbage bag overcoat. This is a cheap yet effective solution to staying relatively dry and a great way of keeping your pants dry when riding the chair. Simply cut a hole in the bottom of a large garbage bag for your head and two armholes in the sides. Voila, you have a functional if not overly fashionable "Bagner" ski suit.

A stormy day on Blackcomb.

- Wear your hood on any lifts that don't have covers and quickly wipe the water off the cushion of the chair lift before you sit down.

- Try to bring a backpack with a spare set of gloves and hat. It can double the amount of time you can enjoy yourself on the hill.

39

Strategies For Skiing On Rainy Days

- Carry a small goggle wiper with you. They are inexpensive and widely available. Use them to keep your goggle lens clear. Also, leave your goggles on your face. If you place your goggles on your forehead the heat from your head will likely cause the lens to fog beyond recovery. A wise friend once said, "Goggles belong on your face or in their case".

- After skiing for the morning head inside to one of the restaurants. Use the glove-dryers that are available free of charge and hang your jacket up so it can drip-dry a little.

- Ski or board for the afternoon or until you get soaked. At this point, head home, hot tub and recite after me … "What a great day!

- When you get home, hang up your clothing. Pull the liners out of your boots and place them a safe distance from a heat source. They should dry overnight. If your clothing was hopelessly insufficient during the day consider renting some higher end garments (from one of several companies in town) for the next day

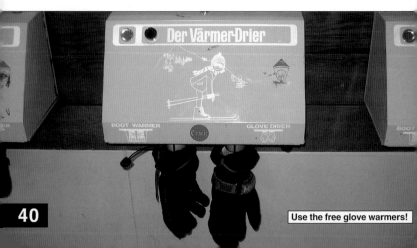

Use the free glove warmers!

Strategies For Skiing Down At The End Of The Day

Physically, all mountains are much bigger at the base. However, from a skiing standpoint, Whistler and Blackcomb are up-side-down pyramids. In other words, there is much more skiing terrain at the top of the mountain than at the bottom. The dynamic created by this fact is the funneling of skiers into only a handful of runs on the lower mountain and, ultimately, into one run near the bottom. Obviously, this creates a high-traffic situation.

Like any high-traffic commute, the problems can be compounded when drivers of all abilities are forced onto the same road. Imagine if all the drivers on a busy road went by different rules. This is some-times what it feels like when you are skiing out at the end of the day. To avoid the potential road rage and stress of this commute, there are a few things that you can do.

It can get pretty hectic at the end of the day.

☐ Avoid the lower-mountain shenanigans altogether! Ride the lift down (download) and watch the madness from above.

☐ Plan to end your day a little earlier or stick around until the crowd dissipates late in the day.

☐ As always, when you stop to rest your legs, it is very important to do so in a suitable spot. Try standing behind one of the "Slow Skiing" banners.

Tips For Riding Lifts

Whistler Blackcomb has a full range of lift types to move people up the hill, including handle tows, magic carpets, T-bars, fixed-grip chairs, detachable chairs, as well as a few different styles of gondolas. Like any machinery, ski lifts can harm you if not used correctly. If you are ever in doubt about how to ride any of the lifts, ask the lift attendant for assistance. Always be mindful of loose clothing, pack straps and ski poles that might get caught when loading or unloading.

T- Bars

Of all the lift types, T-bars seem to cause first-time riders the greatest grief. The most common problems happen when passengers try to <u>sit</u> on the T-bar. Remember to stand up and let the bar drag you, as opposed to being completely supported by it. For best results and comfort, pair up with someone approximately your size. This will allow you to counterbalance one another more efficiently.

Snowboards pose a few more options (and complications) for T-bars. Riding a surface lift on a board is harder than on skis because you have only one foot in a binding. The other foot is loose and placed in front of the rear binding. Some riders prefer to ride alone, because this allows more opportunity to adjust their balance. Others prefer to have someone counterbalance the opposite side of the T. Regardless of which method you choose, you can ride with the T between your legs or behind your hip.

If you are new to riding T-bars, watch other riders carefully, listen to the lift operator's instructions and wait for a quiet day. On busy days with new snow, expert skiers will be anxious to get on the T-bars and access the goods. They will have little patience for people misloading and falling on the track.

🎿 Carpet Tows

Think of these lifts as the mountain equivalent of the moving side-walks at the airport. They are situated in beginner zones and operate at very slow speeds to allow you to step on board.

🎿 Handle Tows

Also used in beginner zones and run at low speeds.

🪑 Fixed-Grip Chair

"Fixed-grip" refers to the fact that the chair is bolted directly onto the cable and that it runs at the same speed throughout the loading, riding and unloading processes. Thus, the chair is often moving at a faster pace when we get on and off the lift in comparison with the detachable lifts we have come to know and love.

🪑 Detachable Chair

"Detachable" means these chairs are mechanically removed from the cable at each station. This technology allows for the cable to run much faster, because the chairs themselves accelerate and decelerate (independent of the cable) to speeds that allow riders to load and unload easily.

🚠 Gondola

Gondolas at Whistler Blackcomb come in several shapes and sizes, but all offer the comfort of travelling uphill while being sheltered from the weather. For the standing-room cabins like the Whistler Village Gondola, you must bring your skis or snowboard inside the cabin with you. For the seat-equipped cabins of the Excalibur and Creekside gondolas, you must slot your skis or board into exterior racks before you climb in and sit down. (Skiers, bring your poles in.) Lift operators are on hand to assist with the loading and unloading of your equipment.

43

Weather

In the Coast Range of British Columbia there are three main weather patterns. Each of them affect the snow conditions. Thankfully, the most common pattern is the southwest flow, which brings moderate temperatures and predictable snow to the mountains. The second is the dreaded Pineapple Express, which brings very moist, warm air up from the subtropics. High freezing levels and rain are associated with a Pineapple Express.

The final pattern is the high-pressure northerly outflow, in which cold air from the arctic flows south and leaves the mountain in a period of drought. Very cold temperatures are likely in the alpine.

Daylight Hours (Valley)

Month	Monthly Average
November	9:52
December	8:29
January	8:17
February	9:25
March	11:00
April	12:53
May	14:36
June	15:57
July	16:10
August	15:08
September	13:28
October	11:40

You don't want to miss this!

Snowfall Averages*

November	88cm	35"
December	284cm	112"
January	183cm	72"
February	109cm	43"
March	198cm	78"
April	118cm	46"
May	53cm	21"

*Measurements taken at 1600m/5249'.

Valley Temperature Averages

Month	High (c)	Low (c)	High (f)	Low (f)
November	+5	-1	+41	+30
December	-1	-5	+30	+23
January	-2	-8	+28	+18
February	+3	-5	+37	+23
March	+8	-3	+46	+27
April	+11	-2	+52	+36
May	+17	+7	+62	+44
June	+21	+9	+70	+48
July	+27	+11	+80	+52
August	+27	+11	+80	+52
September	+20	+8	+65	+46
October	+16	+3	+60	+38

Alpine Temperature Averages

Month	High (c)	Low (c)	High (f)	Low (f)
December	-5	-12	+23	+10
January	-5	-12	+23	+10
February	-5	-12	+23	+10
March	+5	-8	+41	+18
April	+5	-8	+41	+18
May	+5	-8	+41	+18

Here's a good rule of thumb about what air temperature in Vancouver relates to snowfall in Whistler. Typically, if the temperature in Vancouver is 7 degrees Celsius or colder, and it is raining, we will see snow in Whistler Village. If the temperature is 10 degrees in Vancouver, there will be freezing temperatures at the top of the Wizard Chair on Blackcomb.

Check the temperature and precipitation charts in order to get a feel for what you can expect while you are here.

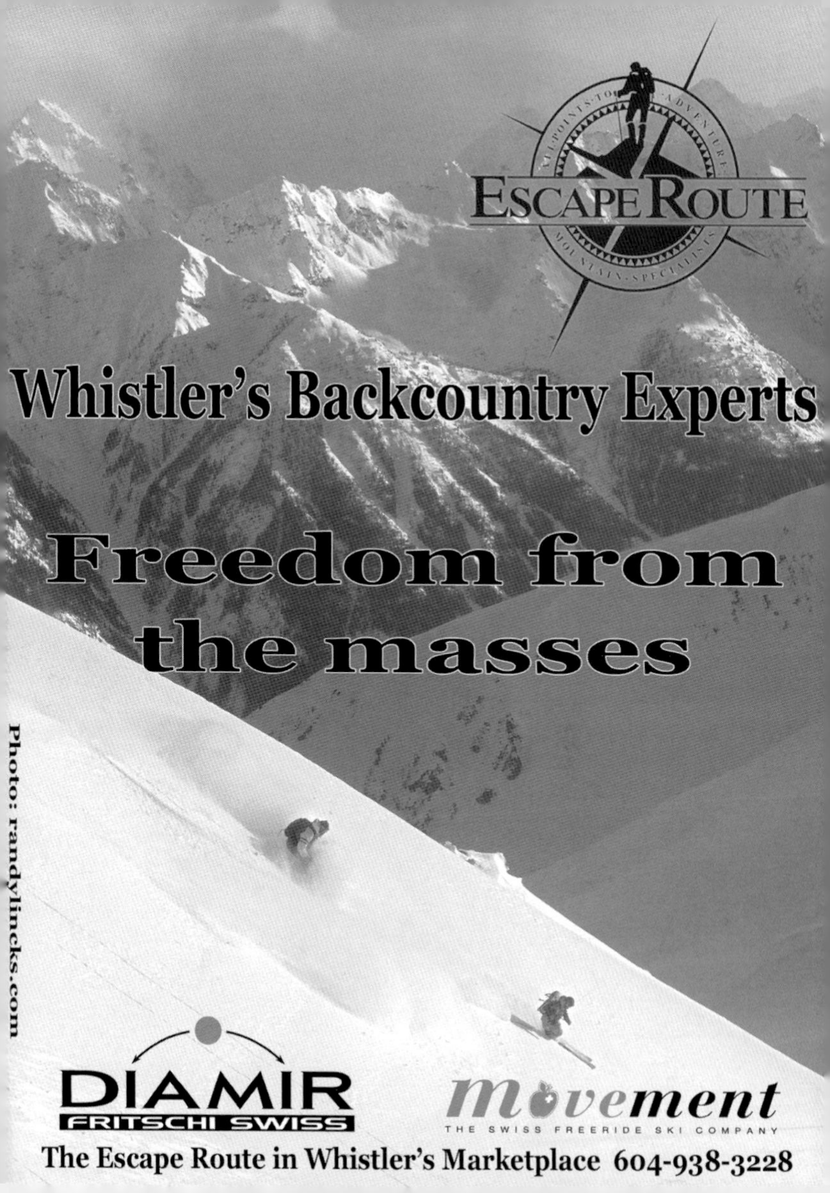

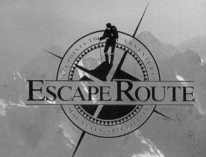

ALL·POINTS·TO·ADVENTURE
ESCAPE ROUTE
MOUNTAIN·SPECIALISTS
Whistler's Backcountry Experts
Freedom from the masses
Photo: randylincks.com
DIAMIR
FRITSCHI SWISS
movement
THE SWISS FREERIDE SKI COMPANY
The Escape Route in Whistler's Marketplace 604-938-3228

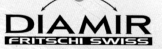

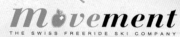

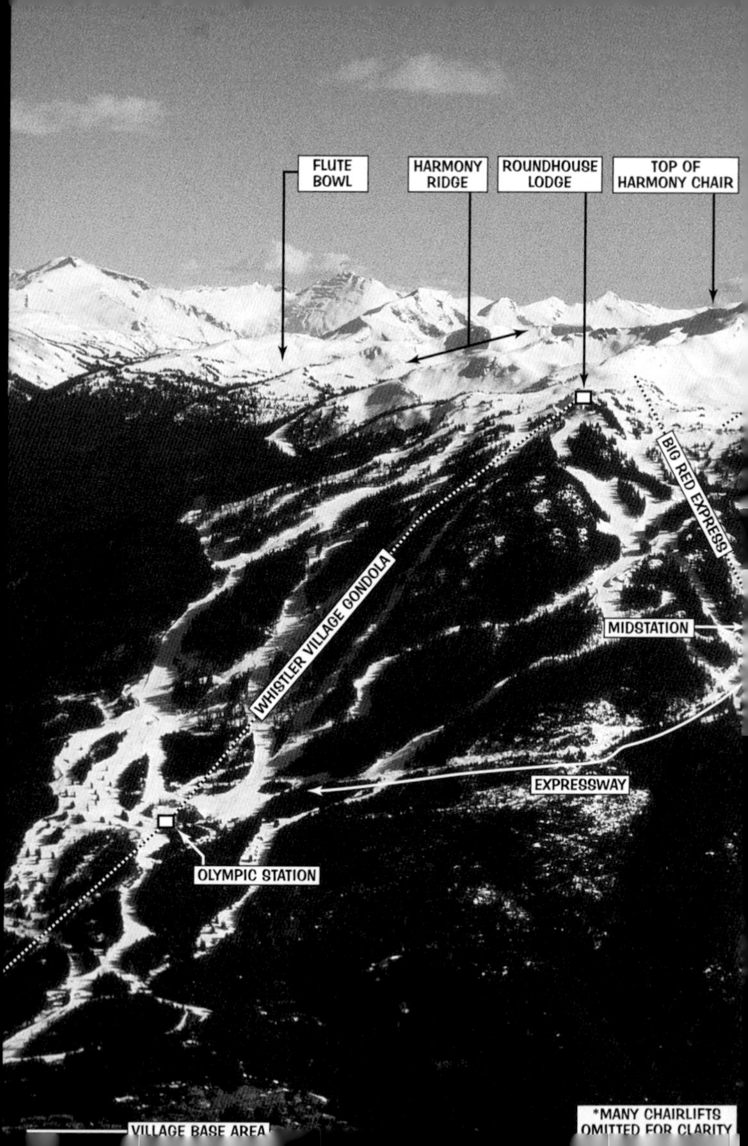

FLUTE BOWL

HARMONY RIDGE

ROUNDHOUSE LODGE

TOP OF HARMONY CHAIR

BIG RED EXPRESS

MIDSTATION

WHISTLER VILLAGE GONDOLA

EXPRESSWAY

OLYMPIC STATION

VILLAGE BASE AREA

*MANY CHAIRLIFTS OMITTED FOR CLARITY

UPPER PEAK
TO CREEK

PEAK CHAIR

HIGHWAY 86

LOWER PEAK TO CREEK

CREEKSIDE GONDOLA

CREEKSIDE BASE AREA

Whistler - Vertical Chart

	Village	Olympic Stn.	Bottom Big Red	Creekside	Harmony Top
Village	0	1157'	20512'	n/a	4725'
Olympic Stn.	1157'	0	919'	n/a	3593'
Bottom Big Red	2051'	919'	0	2113'	2674'
Creekside	n/a	n/a	2113'	0	4779'
Harmony Top	4725'	3593'	2674'	4799'	0
Chicpea Café	3239'	2107'	1188'	3313'	1486'
Roundhouse	3855'	2723'	1804'	3929'	870'
Peak Chair Top	4946'	3814'	2895'	5020'	221'

Chicpea Café	Roundhouse	Peak Chair Top
3239'	3855'	4946'
2107'	2723'	3814'
1188'	1804'	2895'
3313'	3929'	5020'
1486'	870'	221'
0	616'	1707'
616'	0	1091'
1707'	1091'	0

photo: Brian Leighton

photo: Alain Denis

Whistler images clockwise from far left: skiing with views of the Black Tusk, the Roundhouse Lodge, rimed chair, powder cruising and an alpine overview.

Whistler Mountain Familiarization Tour

The following is a self-guided tour recommended for intermediate skiers and snowboarders. It is designed to highlight some of the key lifts and runs and to familiarize visitors to the layout of the mountain.

Start at the lightboard near the top of the Whistler Village Gondola, Emerald Express and Big Red Express on Whistler Mountain.

⇨ Ski down Ego Bowl (skier's left of the Emerald Express chair) to the junction with Enchanted Forest. Ski Enchanted Forest to the bottom of the Emerald Express and ride back up.

⇨ Get off the Emerald Express and turn right. Again, ski down the top pitch of Ego Bowl, but this time merge right onto Cougar. Follow Cougar until it rejoins Ego Bowl and ski back down to the bottom of the Emerald Express. Ride the chair back up.

⇨ Get off the Emerald Express and turn right. Ski down Whiskey Jack to the bottom of the Emerald Express. This time, however, continue down Upper Olympic Run to the bottom of the Garbanzo Express. LOOK CAREFULLY FOR THE LEFT HAND TURN TOWARDS THE GARBANZO EXPRESS. DON'T SKI ALL THE WAY TO THE GONDOLA. Ride up the Garbanzo Express.

⇨ Get off the Garbanzo Express and turn right. Ski Orange Peel to Bear Cub. Ski Bear Cub to the base of the Big Red Express. Ride up the Big Red Express.

⇨ Get off the Big Red Express and head back towards the lightboard where you started. From the lightboard, ski Pony Trail all the way to the bottom of the Big Red Express and ride back up.

⇨ Get off the Big Red and ski over to the <u>top</u> of the Emerald Express. Ski Marmot to the base of the Harmony Express. Ride up the Harmony Express.

➡ Get off the Harmony Express and turn left. Ski Harmony Ridge to the bottom of the Harmony Express. Ride back up the Harmony Express.

➡ Get off the Harmony Express and go straight, eventually turning left and skiing the Burnt Stew Trail to the bottom of the Harmony Express. Ride back up the Harmony Express.

➡ Get off the Harmony Express and go straight, eventually turning right to the entrance to The Saddle. Ski the Saddle to the bottom of the T-Bars. Ride up the T-bar.

➡ Get off the T-Bar and turn right. Ski T-bar Run (skier's left of the T-bars). Continue past the bottom of the T-bars to the junction with Pony Trail. Ski Pony Trail to the bottom of the Big Red Express and ride back up the lift.

You are now back to where you started. Hopefully you feel more familiar with Whistler Mountain.

Whistler Village Gondola Overview

BOTTOM OF EMERALD EXPRESS

33

PTARMIGAN

32

UPPER OLYMPIC

4   5

UPPER FANTASTIC

OLYMPIC STATION

1

LOWER FANTASTIC

WHISTLER VILLAGE GONDOLA

FITZSIMMONS EXPRESS

TOP OF GARBANZO EXPRESS

TOP OF PEAK CHAIR

35

BEAR PAW

36

TOKUM

27

BOTTOM OF GARBANZO EXPRESS

TOP OF FITZSIMMONS EXPRESS

EXPRESSWAY

LOWER OLYMPIC

CRABAPPLE

2

3

Whistler Mountain

UPPER FANTASTIC

BOTTOM OF OLYMPIC CHAIR

OLYMPIC STATION

BOTTOM OF GARBANZO EXPRESS

TOP OF FITZSIMMONS EXPRESS

CRABAPPLE

LOWER OLYMPIC

LOWER FANTASTIC

Lower Whistler Village Gondola / Fitzsimmons Express Chair

There are some decent runs in this zone, but timing is everything. Avoid this zone if:

☐ There is a large line at the Whistler Village Gondola and Fitzsimmons Express chair.

☐ It's the end of the day, and everyone is heading down to the village.

☐ It's raining in the valley. Head up to higher zones, where it's probably snowing!

Conversely, this can be a decent zone to ski if none of the above criteria are present.

1. Lower Fantastic
Starts at the bottom of the Olympic Chair. Additional photo on page 54.

2. Lower Olympic
Starts at Olympic Station. Additional photo on page 55.

3. Crabapple
Can be accessed from either Expressway or the top of the Fitzsimmons Express. Additional photos on pages 55 and 77. **Please note**, the best way to ski this zone is a combination of Lower Olympic and Lower Fantastic. From Olympic Station, ski Lower Olympic to Lower Fantastic. Follow Fantastic until it is possible to rejoin Olympic and follow it to the valley.

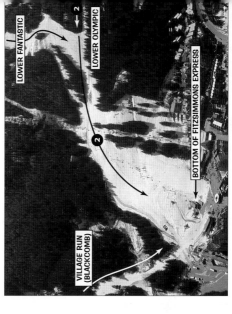

LOWER FANTASTIC

LOWER OLYMPIC

VILLAGE RUN (BLACKCOMB)

BOTTOM OF FITZSIMMONS EXPRESS

Olympic Chair

This is the best zone for beginners! Aside from the Olympic Chair itself, there is a Carpet Tow and two handle tows at the Children's Learning Centre.

4. Upper Fantastic . . . .
Not quite fantastic…but pretty good! Additional photos on pages 54 and 56.

5. Upper Olympic (lower section beside chair) . . . . .
If you are a beginner skier or boarder, this is for you! Additional photos on pages 54 and 56.

6. It Happens . . . .
"It happens" to be heavily used by skiers of all abilities to access the Garbanzo Express and the Whistler Village Gondola. It is recommended to use this run only for this purpose.

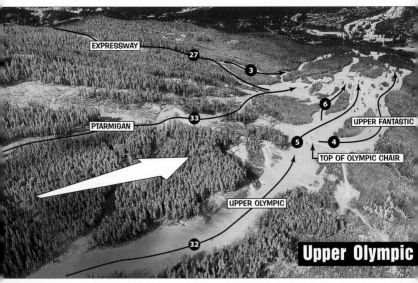

Upper Olympic

Olympic Chair

32

33

UPPER OLYMPIC

PTARMIGAN

TOP OF OLYMPIC CHAIR

4

5 6

UPPER FANTASTIC

UPPER OLYMPIC

IT HAPPENS

CHILDREN'S LEARNING CENTRE

CARPET TOW

OLYMPIC STATION

BOTTOM OF OLYMPIC CHAIR

59

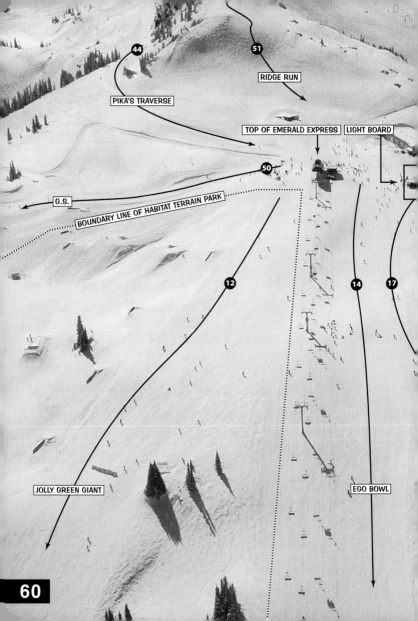

44

51

RIDGE RUN

PIKA'S TRAVERSE

TOP OF EMERALD EXPRESS

LIGHT BOARD

50

G.S.

BOUNDARY LINE OF HABITAT TERRAIN PARK

12

14

17

JOLLY GREEN GIANT

EGO BOWL

30

20

BOTTOM OF T-BARS

BOTTOM OF PEAK CHAIR

LITTLE RED RUN

PONY TRAIL

ROUNDHOUSE LODGE

TOP OF WHISTLER VILLAGE GONDOLA

UPPER WHISKEY JACK

Emerald Express Overview

MARMOT

GREEN ACRES

BOBCAT

COYOTE

JOLLY GREEN GIANT

BOUNDARY OF HABITAT TERRAIN PARK

PONTIAC RACE CENTRE

SIDEWINDER

TOP OF EMERALD EXPRESS

15 COUGAR

14 EGO BOWL

17 UPPER WHISKEY JACK

CHIC PEA CAFE

16

18

PIG ALLEY

17

ENCHANTED FOREST

19

LOWER WHISKEY JACK

OLD CROW

33

33

PTARMIGAN

PTARMIGAN

BOTTOM OF EMERALD EXPRESS

Emerald Express Chair

The Emerald Express Chair is the main stomping grounds for lower-end intermediate skiers and boarders. It services a selection of classic groomed runs, a family zone, a terrain park and a half pipe, all at an elevation that preserves snow quality. It's only downside is that it is often one of the most crowded lifts on both mountains.

The latest management plan at Whistler Mountain places Green Acres and Jolly Green Giant within the confines of the Habitat Terrain Park. Truly a sign of the times; the needs of the skiing public have shifted away from groomed runs toward that of created jumps and features. Skiers and boarders are still allowed to cruise Green Acres and Jolly Green Giant, but should be cognizant to the fact that the principal purpose of these runs revolves around the park.

7. Marmot . . . .
This run is really just a service road from the top of Emerald Express to the bottom of Harmony Express. It is not recommended for any other purpose. More photos on pages 62, 89, 91 & 95.

8. Sidewinder . . . .
Also known as Mindbender! This painfully flat run is an important thoroughfare allowing you to get over to the bottom of the Emerald Express (or lower) from the base of the Harmony Express. Additional photos on pages 62, 89 and 91.

9. Habitat Terrain Park . . . .
After the Big Easy Terrain Park on Blackcomb, this is the second most accommodating park for riders making a transition over to the dark side of freestyle! Have a slide through the park and check out all of the features. On your next run, tailor your choice of boxes, rails and table tops to suit your ability. Enjoy! Additional photos on pages 60 and 62.

10. Green Acres . . . .
This run is now part of the Habitat Terrain Park. Look around the sides of the park features for some fresh grooming or pockets of powder but watch out for those freestylers!

11. Coyote . . . .
An alternative ending to Green Acres. Would be really nice if it didn't have a flat road cutting across the middle of it! Additional photo on page 62.

12. Jolly Green Giant . . . .
A beautifully varied run within the Habitat Terrain Park. Steeper sections are broken up by flatter sections that give your legs a break! Additional photos on pages 60, 62 and 67 and 95.

TOP OF EMERALD EXPRESS
ROUNDHOUSE LODGE

Green Acres

12

10

7

MARMOT

JOLLY GREEN GIANT

GREEN ACRES

13

9

BOBCAT

BOUNDARY LINE OF HABITAT TERRAIN PARK

11

COYOTE

8

SIDEWINDER

65

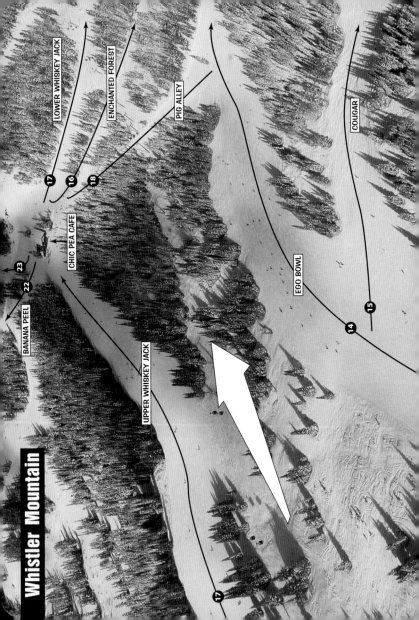

Whistler Mountain

LOWER WHISKEY JACK

ENCHANTED FOREST

PIG ALLEY

COUGAR

CHIC PEA CAFE

EGO BOWL

BANANA PEEL

UPPER WHISKEY JACK

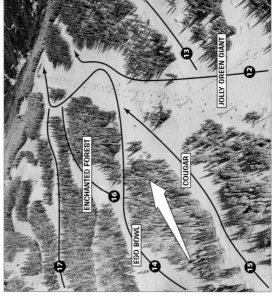

13. Bobcat ....

An alternative ending to Jolly Green Giant. Additional photos on pages 62 and 65.

14. Ego Bowl ....

A time-earned classic. Gentle, winding terrain. Additional photos on pages 60 and 63.

15. Cougar ....

By skiing Ego Bowl to Cougar, you can mix in one pitch of Blue skiing to your Green run. Additional photo on page 63.

16. Enchanted Forest ....

Nice cruising. Can be accessed by either Ego Bowl or at the bottom of Lower Whiskey Jack. Additional photo on page 63.

17. Upper and ....
Lower Whiskey Jack

Classic wide cruising run. Upper Whiskey Jack is the section above the Chic Pea café. The "Lower" run refers the section from the Chic Pea to the bottom of the Emerald Express. Additional photos on pages 61, 63 and 68.

18. Pig Alley ....

Just a sneak route to get from Whiskey Jack to Ego Bowl. Additional photo on page 63.

19. Old Crow ....

A nice variation from skiing the standard Lower Whiskey Jack. Look for the signs and avoid getting drawn down Ptarmigan (Blue) if you want to get back to Emerald Express! Photo on page 63.

Whistler Mountain

ROUNDHOUSE LODGE

TOP OF GARBANZO EXPRESS

PAPOOSE

BEAR CUB

PONY TRAIL

BANANA PEEL

ORANGE PEEL

DAVE MURRAY DOWNHILL

20

21

24

17

24

22

23

34

Big Red Express Chair

The Big Red offers access to classic runs on a wide variety of terrain.

Tree Fort

20. Pony Trail . . . .

With apologies to Lennon and McCartney, this is truly a long and winding road. Although there are many flat sections on this run, there are two steep pitches that many believe should be rated Blue. Specifically, the pitch directly off the top (below the lightboard) and the section that passes under the Big Red Express are uncharacteristically steep in comparison to the rest of the run. Additional photo on page 73.

21. Bear Cub . . .

This is a great run for parents with young children, because you can pull over at the awesome Tree Fort Fun Park. There are two tree houses, a slide and picnic tables at the park! Additional photo on page 70.

22. Banana Peel . . . .

A short but sweet run. Access from Upper Whiskey Jack and turning skiers' left above the Chic Pea Café. From the bottom of Banana Peel, take either Pony Trail or Bear Cub to reach the bottom of the Big Red Express. Additional photo on page 66.

23. Orange Peel . . . .

A short run but a stellar slope. Often much less crowded than the runs over at the Emerald Express. Access by skiing to the right off the top of the Garbanzo Express. Hook up with either Pony Trail (Green) or Bear

Cub (Green) to get to the Big Red Express. Additional photos on pages 66 and 71.

Whistler Mountain

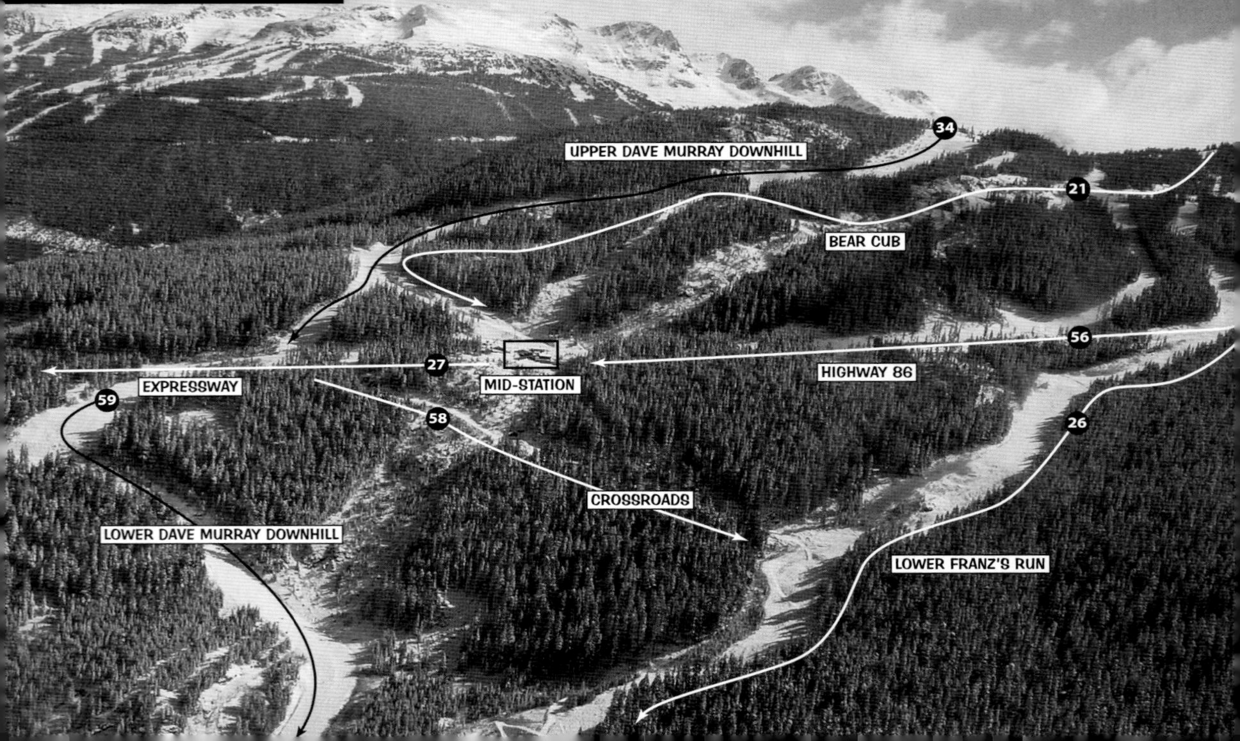

UPPER DAVE MURRAY DOWNHILL

BEAR CUB

HIGHWAY 86

LOWER FRANZ'S RUIN

CROSSROADS

MID-STATION

EXPRESSWAY

LOWER DAVE MURRAY DOWNHILL

21

34

56

26

27

58

59

24. Papoose ....

A flat run most often used to link Upper Whiskey Jack and Upper Pony Trail with Bear Cub or Upper Franz's Run. Photo on page 68.

25. Upper Franz's Run ....

A favorite run to some and a real enigma to others! Many intermediate skiers find this run very challenging and intimidating, as it can be extremely busy and turn into a mogul run/skating rink by mid-morning. It is best skied early in the day on fresh grooming. Enjoy! Additional photo on page 105.

26. Lower Franz's Run

The continuation of Franz's from its intersection with Highway 86. A mega-classic cruiser and a must-do for advanced intermediate skiers! Crowded and bumpy at the end of the day. Additional photos on pages 104 and 105.

27. Expressway ....

It is an important route to allow skiers from the bottom of the Big Red Express to get over to the Garbanzo Express, Whistler Village Gondola, Cross Roads (Blue) and the ski runs down to Whistler Village. Don't expect good skiing on Expressway. Additional photos on pages 48, 55, 58, 76, 77, 104 and 105.

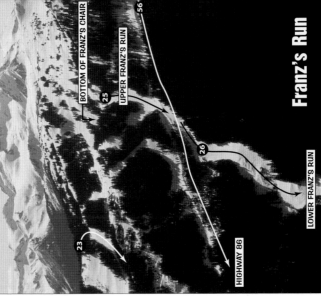

Franz's Run

 **Franz's Chair**

This chair only operates during the busiest periods, such as Christmas and spring break. You can bypass it by skiing down to the bottom of the Big Red Express. To access the Big Red Express from the bottom of Franz's Chair, however, you must either ski the steep, intimidating Upper Franz's (Blue+) or step up a short slope to access Bear Cub (Green).

28. Porcupine ....
A very wide run that usually sees little traffic.

29. Fisheye ....
Nothing fishy about this. A nice run with a couple of steep rollovers. Access from Pony Trail (Green).

30. Little Red Run ....
Good skiing.

31. Old Man ....
Old Man refers to the expanse of terrain on the skier's left of Franz's Chair. It can be a good adventure, even for a young man!

ROUNDHOUSE LODGE

20

30

Franz's Chair

PONY TRAIL

29

LITTLE RED

28

PORCUPINE

FISH EYE

◆

BOTTOM OF FRANZ'S CHAIR

Garbanzo Express Chair

A great alternative to riding the Emerald Express or Big Red Express. The crowds rarely find this lift!

32. Upper Olympic . . . .

A great, wide run. Many believe that Upper Olympic could be rated Blue, as it is fairly steep in places. It is often very crowded at the end of the day, when skiers are descending to the village. Additional photos on pages 54, 58 and 59.

33. Ptarmigan . . . .

A step up in difficulty from the runs over at the Emerald Express, and as a result, often much less congested. Many intermediate skiers find the section near the bottom of Seppos (Black), about halfway down, to be intimidating! Additional photos on pages 54, 58 , 59, 63, 76 and 77.

Access: From the top of the Garbanzo Express, ski down toward the Chic Pea Café and continue on Lower Whiskey Jack. Look for the Ptarmigan signs on your left.

34. Upper Dave Murray Downhill

The site of the 2010 Olympic Men's Downhill event. Murray himself was a "Crazy Canuck" and Whistler icon who earned his reputation on steep runs like his namesake. Additional photos on pages 68, 70, 77, 104 and 105.

Ptarmigan

TOP OF GARBANZO EXPRE

33

33

PTARMIGAN

BOTTOM OF EMERALD EXPRESS

32

33

UPPER OLYMPIC

PTARMIGAN

Garbanzo Express Cha

35. Bear Paw . . . .

Access this run from Dave Murray Downhill. Additional photo on page 55.

36. Tokum . . . .

You need to ski a short section of the steep, Upper Dave Murray Downhill (Black) to reach Tokum. If you are up to it, it's worth it! Additional photo on page 55.

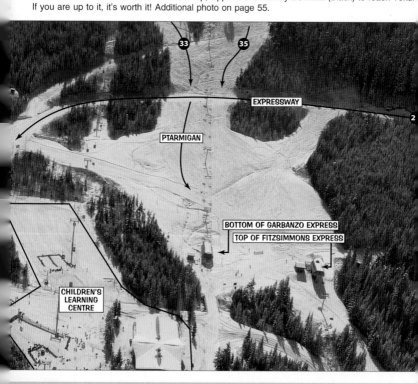

Tokum

34

UPPER DAVE MURRAY
DOWNHILL (HIDDEN IN TREES)

35   36

BEAR PAW

TOKUM

27

EXPRESSWAY

33

3

TARMIGAN

CRABAPPLE

77

BOTTOM OF GARBANZO EXPRESS

Whistler Mountain

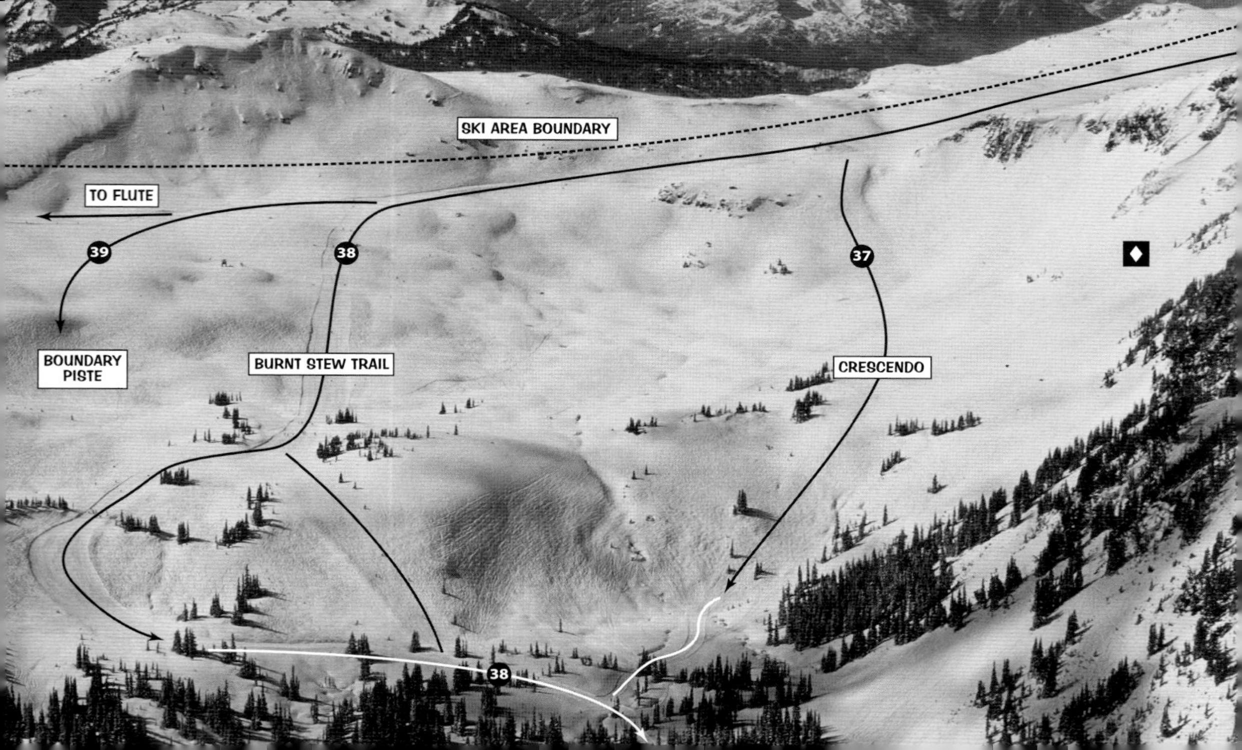

CRESCENDO

37

SKI AREA BOUNDARY

38

38

BURNT STEW TRAIL

TO FLUTE

39

BOUNDARY PISTE

Harmony Express Chair

Many people's favorite lift on Whistler Mountain. It provides access to many exciting runs for skiers of intermediate and expert ability. It is often one of the two busiest lifts (along with Emerald Express) on Whistler.

To access the Symphony Bowl Zone, ski straight once you get off the top of the Harmony Express chair, past the ski patrol shack on your right. Look for the signs and follow the Burnt Stew Trail (Green) to the top of Symphony Bowl.

Note: All runs in this zone require skiing or snowboarding on flat sections of road. Intermediate snowboarders may find these sections of road to be particularly arduous. When foggy, the visibility in this zone is incredibly poor because there are very few trees to give reference.

37. Crescendo . . . . ☐ 🔲 💥 2 💥 🔵🗻 📷 🏔️ ☐

A nice long run off the beaten track. Advanced intermediates may make the most out of their trips to Symphony Bowl by choosing Crescendo.

38. Burnt Stew Trail . . ☐ ⚫ 💥 3 💥 ▨▨ 🔵🗻 📷 🏔️ 🟢 ☐

The easiest route down Symphony Bowl. A great way to get into a spectacular alpine setting while staying on an easy run. There are opportunities to step off the groomed run and try your hand

at some gentle powder skiing. Because this is the easiest run in the zone, there are high-visibility piste markers along the side of the run. Additional photos on pages 80, 81, 87 and 88.

39. Boundary Piste . . . ☐ 💥 2 💥 🔵🗻 📷 🏔️ ☐

This run allows you to explore the outer limits of Symphony Bowl but it does not get regular grooming. Refer to the grooming maps for its daily condition. Boundary Piste affords spectacular views and great opportunities to enjoy gentle powder slopes. Additional photo on page 87.

To access Boundary Piste, follow Burnt Stew Trail to the point where it heads down into Symphony Bowl. Continue sliding out toward a large, wooden sign and fence line, indicating the entrance to the Flute Zone. For Boundary Piste, turn down hill into Symphony Bowl before the fence line.

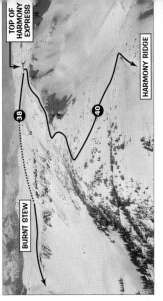

TOP OF HARMONY EXPRESS

BURNT STEW

38

40

HARMONY RIDGE

Harmony Express Chair

40. Harmony Ridge . . . .

This run puts you in a spectacular situation but is a main artery for expert skiers to access Black Diamond runs. Because of this, it's very busy at the top and can be intimidating for intermediates. The top of the run often gets "bumped up" quickly because of heavy traffic. More photos on pages 79 & 88.

41. The Glades . . . .

A nice pitch near the end of Harmony Ridge. Ride Harmony Ridge until you reach "The Glades" sign directing you to the right.

42. Krummholz . . . .

A contrived run that allows you to bail off Harmony Ridge onto Harmony Piste. Photo on page 88.

TOP OF HARMONY EXPRESS

Harmony Ridge

HARMONY RIDGE

THE GLADES

BURNT STEW TRAIL

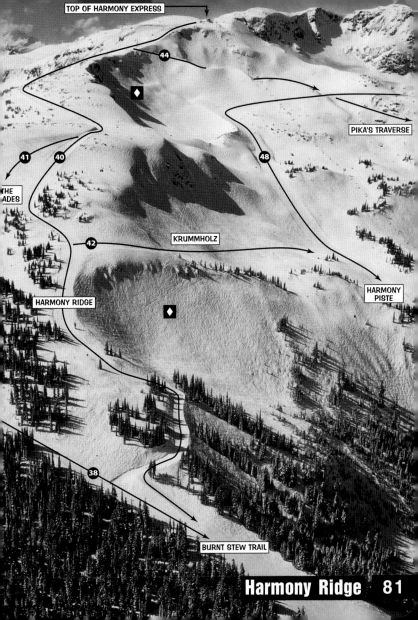

TOP OF HARMONY EXPRESS

44

PIKA'S TRAVERSE

41

40

48

THE
ADES

KRUMMHOLZ

42

HARMONY
PISTE

HARMONY RIDGE

38

BURNT STEW TRAIL

Harmony Ridge 81

════════ **Harmony Express Chair**

43. The Saddle . . . .

A stunning line down the heart of Glacier Bowl and a true Whistler classic. It can, however, be intimidating at the top where it's steep and narrow. Once past this top section, it widens into a beautiful cruising run. There are lots of places where you can traverse off the groomed track into the bowl to sample the powder. Additional photos on pages 88, 92, 94 and 97.

44. Pika's Traverse . . . .

A useful run to access the Lower Harmony Zone or get back to the Roundhouse Zone. It also allows access to some relatively gentle powder slopes near the Camel Backs (Black). Additional photos on pages 60, 81, 89, 90, 91, 92 and 94.

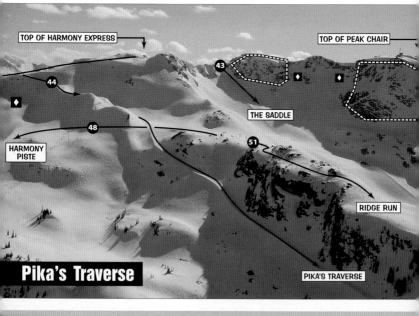

TOP OF HARMONY EXPRESS

TOP OF PEAK CHAIR

43

THE SADDLE

44

48

HARMONY PISTE

51

RIDGE RUN

Pika's Traverse

PIKA'S TRAVERSE

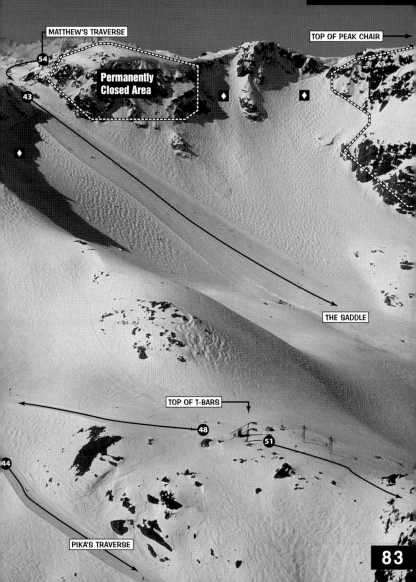

MATTHEW'S TRAVERSE

TOP OF PEAK CHAIR →

54

Permanently Closed Area

43

THE SADDLE

TOP OF T-BARS

48

51

44

PIKA'S TRAVERSE

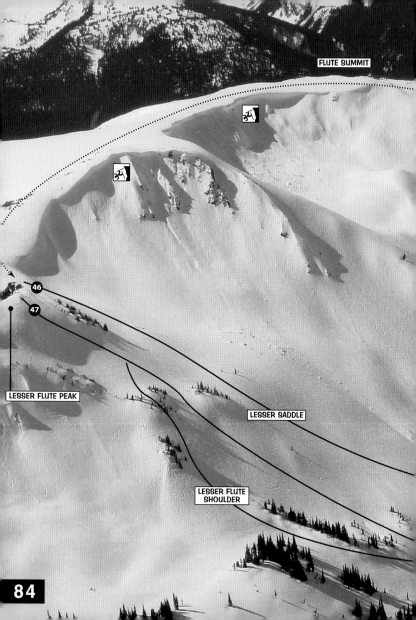

FLUTE SUMMIT

46

47

LESSER FLUTE PEAK

LESSER SADDLE

LESSER FLUTE
SHOULDER

Flute Bowl Overview

TRAVERSE FROM BOUNDARY PISTE

45

EASY
ROUTE

 ## Harmony Express Chair

The promotional material will tell you that Flute Bowl is 700 acres of heavenly terrain. Although this is true, it comes with a cautionary statement. Flute Bowl is a "backcountry-style" experience, meaning there is no direct lift access and are no signs marking the runs. People accessing this area must be able to recognize the terrain that is suitable for their ability level!

Most of the runs in this zone require a steep, grueling hike for access, and all runs require hiking and flat traverses to exit. It is strongly recommended that any skier entering Flute Bowl be a conditioned athlete with experience skiing in big mountains. That being said, there is some beautiful intermediate terrain.

Access: From the top of the Harmony Express Chair, follow Burnt Stew Trail to Boundary Piste. Avoid skiing down Boundary Piste and look east for a large wooden sign which is the Flute Bowl Avalanche Control Gate. After skiing the run of your choice, follow the piste markers back to the Burnt Stew Trail.

45. Easy Route . . . .
The only run in the zone that requires little or no hiking to access. It does, of course, require a hike/traverse back to the Burnt Stew Piste after descending. Leave yourself a solid 30 to 45 minutes to ski and hike out from the Easy Route! Additional photo on page 85.

46. Lesser Saddle . . . .
A great run requiring a considerable hike (almost 200 meters / 650 feet of elevation gain). The hike up alone requires a minimum of 40 minutes.

Access: From the Flute Bowl Avalanche Control Gate, traverse to the west ridge of Flute Peak and begin the steep climb to the top of the peak. Staying well back from the corniced edge of the bowl, descend to the saddle between Flute Peak and Lesser Flute Peak. The run starts at this saddle. Leave yourself 30 minutes hike/traverse back to Burnt Stew Trail after skiing Lesser Saddle. Additional photo on page 84.

47. Lesser Flute Shoulder . . . .
This is an expanse of terrain that offers exciting options, some of them in the intermediate grade.

Access: From Lesser Saddle, hike up to the top of Lesser Flute Peak and descend to the shoulder. See photo. Leave yourself 30 minutes to hike/traverse back to Burnt Stew Trail after riding the run. Additional photo on page 84.

ATTENTION

EXIT ROUTE FROM FLUTE BASIN

Follow red markers to Burnt Stew Trail

Flute Approach

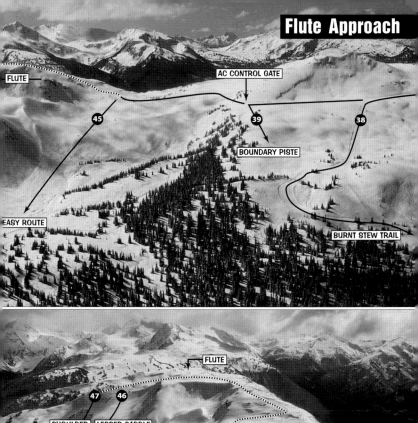

FLUTE

AC CONTROL GATE

45

39

38

BOUNDARY PISTE

EASY ROUTE

BURNT STEW TRAIL

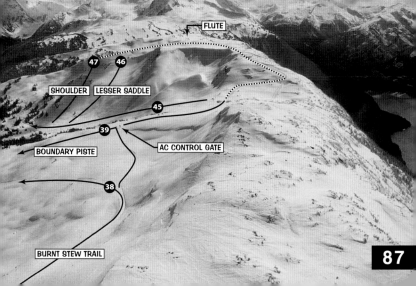

FLUTE

47 46

SHOULDER LESSER SADDLE

45

39

BOUNDARY PISTE

AC CONTROL GATE

38

BURNT STEW TRAIL

Harmony Bowl Overview

40

42

HARMONY RIDGE

KRUMMHOLZ

38

BURNT STEW TRAIL

8

BOTTOM OF HARMONY EXPRESS

TOP OF HARMONY EXPRESS

THE SADDLE

43

44

TOP OF T-BARS

48

44

HARMONY PISTE

PIKA'S TRAVERSE

G.S.

50

MARMOT 7

SIDEWINDER

89

T-Bars

The T-Bars were the original alpine lifts at the resort and still provide efficient access to several great runs.

48. Harmony Piste . . . .
A great run down Harmony Bowl. Advanced intermediate riders may choose to turn down the final pitch of G.S. (above the Harmony Express loading area) instead of following the narrow cat track from this point. Additional photos on pages 81, 82, 83 and 89.

49. Rabbit Tracks . . . .
This great slope is best accessed from Pika's Traverse. It's a good place to find powder (sometimes well after the storm) on a moderate slope.

50. G.S. . . . .
A run with a dual personality. Gentle and meandering at the top yet steep and intimidating above the Harmony Express loading area. Timid skiers can avoid this final slope by following Harmony Piste from this point. Additional photos on pages 60, 89 and 94.

Rabbit Tracks

G.S.

51

44

50

TOP OF EMERALD EXPRESS

ROUNDHOUSE LODGE

48

HARMONY PISTE

7

BURNT STEW TRAIL

G.S.

MARMOT

38

SIDEWINDER

8

BOTTOM OF HARMONY EXPRESS

91

51. Ridge Run......................................

This is a good run on which to return to the Roundhouse area. A short climb uphill from the top of the T-Bars, followed by a traverse along the ridge provides access to Ridge Run. Additional photos on pages 60, 82, 83 and 91.

52. Headwall..

A fairly adventurous run next to the T-Bars. Choose your line carefully, as the top is quite rocky!

53. T-Bar Run.......................................

The only negative about this slope is that it's too short! There are many opportunities to slip off the piste and enjoy some powder in T-Bar Bowl (Black)!

Ridge Run

TOP OF HARMONY EXPRESS

TOP OF T-BARS

51

TOP OF BIG RED EXPRESS

TOP OF FRANZ'S CHAIR

52

53

43

HEADWALL

T-BAR RUN

BOTTOM OF T-BARS

BOTTOM OF PEAK CHAIR

Whistler Peak Overview

TOP OF HARMONY EXPRESS

MATTHEW'S TRAVERSE (HIDDEN)

44

43

THE SADDLE

PIKA'S TRAVERSE

G.S.

TOP OF PEAK CHAIR

54

55

UPPER PEAK TO CREEK (HIDDEN)

Permanently Closed Area

◆

◆

TOP OF EMERALD EXPRESS

ROUNDHOUSE LODGE

TOP OF WHISTLER VILLAGE GONDOLA

50

10

12

BOUNDARY LINE OF HABITAT TERRAIN PARK

7

MARMOT

JOLLY GREEN GIANT

GREEN ACRES

═══════════════════════════════════ **Peak Chair**

This zone is hallowed ground for expert skiers at the resort. In good weather and conditions, however, it does provide some opportunities for intermediate riders.

Note: If the orange light is flashing at the Peak Chair loading area, then the Ski Patrol is recommending that only Expert and Advanced skiers access the Peak Zone. Please trust their judgement. Intermediate skiers and boarders should not ride the Peak Chair if the orange light is flashing!

54. Matthew's Traverse . . . .
Consider this run a feeder route to The Saddle (and some Double Black Diamond runs in Glacier Bowl). Don't expect good skiing until you get to the Saddle. Additional photos on pages 83 and 94.

Peak Unload

55

TOP OF PEAK CHAIR ↓ ◆

UPPER PEAK TO CREEK

54

MATTHEW'S TRAVERSE

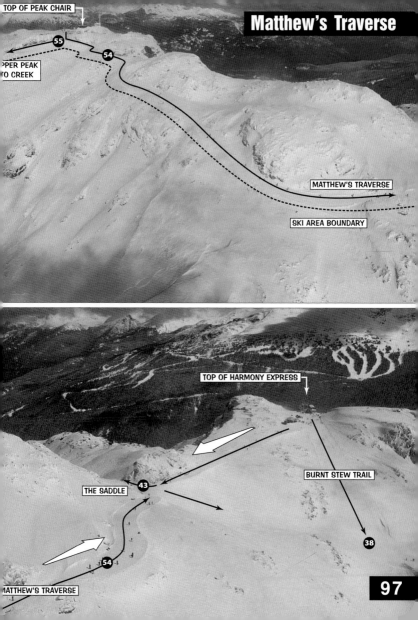

TOP OF PEAK CHAIR

Matthew's Traverse

55

54

PPER PEAK
O CREEK

MATTHEW'S TRAVERSE

SKI AREA BOUNDARY

TOP OF HARMONY EXPRESS

BURNT STEW TRAIL

THE SADDLE

43

38

54

MATTHEW'S TRAVERSE

UPPER PEAK TO CREEK

55

Permanently
Closed Area

WEST BOWL

56

57

HIGHWAY 86

LOWER PEAK TO CREEK

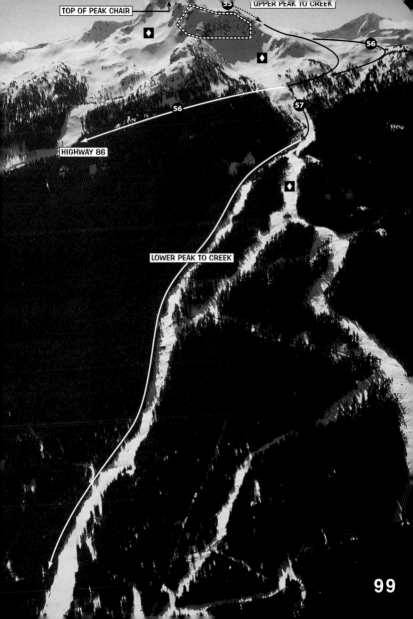

TOP OF PEAK CHAIR

UPPER PEAK TO CREEK

56

56

HIGHWAY 86

57

LOWER PEAK TO CREEK

99

55. Upper Peak To Creek ....

There is some nice riding on this run, but it's true value lies in allowing intermediate skiers into a stunning alpine setting. Once the piste has taken you into Bagel Bowl, there are opportunities to head off the groomed track and onto some gentle powder slopes. Additional photos on pages 49, 95, 96, 97, 98, 99 and 105.

56. Highway 86 ....

It gets a star because of the views alone! More photos on pages 49, 70, 71, 98, 99, 104 & 105.

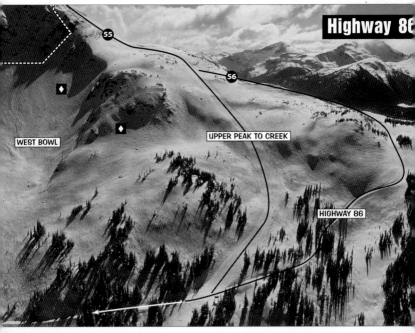

WEST BOWL

UPPER PEAK TO CREEK

HIGHWAY 86

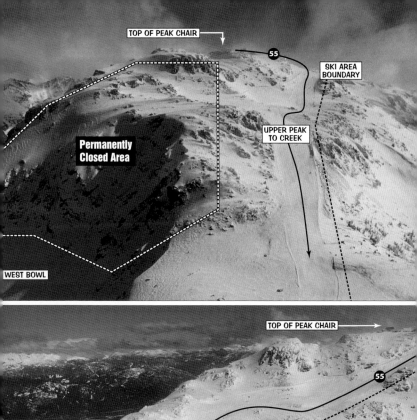

TOP OF PEAK CHAIR

55

SKI AREA BOUNDARY

UPPER PEAK TO CREEK

Permanently Closed Area

WEST BOWL

TOP OF PEAK CHAIR

55

UPPER PEAK TO CREEK

SKI AREA BOUNDARY

Upper Peak to Creek

Whistler Mountain

Peak Chair

You are committed to skiing all of the way down to the Creekside if you head down Lower Peak to Creek!

57. Lower Peak to Creek . . . .

This significant run became an instant classic after it was opened in 2005. It descends 1555 meters (5,020 feet) of vertical from Highway 86 to the Creekside. This run is such a "leg-burner" that there are benches halfway down so the weary can rest! Access by skiing Upper Peak to Creek to Highway 86. Additional photos on pages 49, 98, 99 and 105.

Lower Peak to Creek

WHISTLER CREEKSIDE

LOWER PEAK TO CREEK

57

LOWER PEAK TO CREEK

57

LOWER PEAK TO CREEK

The beauty of the Creekside Gondola is that it is your first opportunity to get out of your car and up the hill if you are arriving from Vancouver. It is often less busy than the gondolas in the village and links directly with the Big Red Express.

58. Cross Roads . . . .

This is a very useful access run for intermediate skiers. Cross Roads allows you to get from Midstation (bottom of Big Red / top of Creekside Gondola) to Lower Franz's and follow a Blue run all the way to the valley (Creekside). To access Cross Roads, head down Expressway and immediately look for the signs pointing to the left. Additional photo on page 70.

59. Lower Dave Murray Downhill . . . .

An exciting run! Best for intermediate skiers to avoid it at the end of the day when it is busy and rough. Additional photo on page 70.

Cross Roads

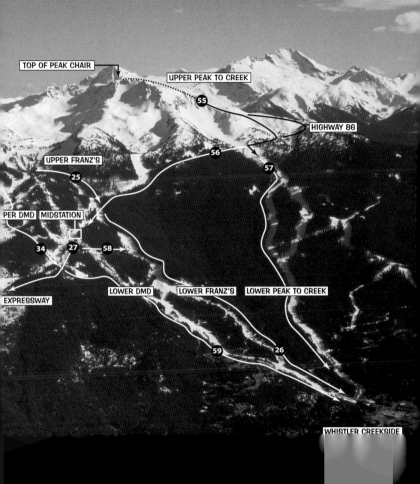

Lower Dave Murray Downhill

TOP OF PEAK CHAIR

UPPER PEAK TO CREEK

55

HIGHWAY 86

56

UPPER FRANZ'S

25

57

PER DMD   MIDSTATION

34   27   58

LOWER DMD   LOWER FRANZ'S   LOWER PEAK TO CREEK

EXPRESSWAY

59   26

WHISTLER CREEKSIDE

Sushilicious

Whistler's Favorite Sushi Restaurant

In the Summit Lodge, Main St.

Lunch (call for hours)

Dinner from 5:00

Take-out available

604.935.5649

Best New Restaurant 2003
Best Sushi 2003 & 2004

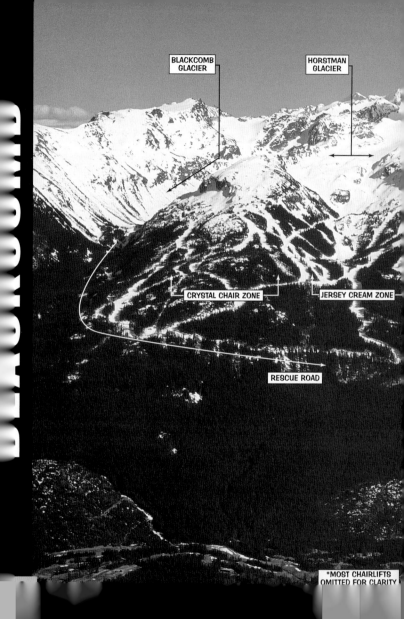

BLACKCOMB

BLACKCOMB GLACIER

HORSTMAN GLACIER

CRYSTAL CHAIR ZONE

JERSEY CREAM ZONE

RESCUE ROAD

*MOST CHAIRLIFTS OMITTED FOR CLARITY

SEVENTH
HEAVEN ZONE

RENDEZVOUS
RESTAURANT

SOLAR COASTER

SUNSET BOULEVARD

WIZARD EXPRESS

BLACKCOMB BASE AREA

BLACKCOMB

Blackcomb - Vertical Chart

	Village	Daylodge	Base 2	Excelerator	Wizard Top
Village	0	n/a	279'	1493'	1882'
Daylodge	n/a	0	246'	1460'	1849'
Base 2	279'	246'	0	1214'	1603'
Excelerator	1493'	1460'	1214'	0	389'
Midstation	1882'	1849'	1603'	389'	0
Rendezvous	3888'	3855'	3669'	2395'	2066'
Glacier Creek	2855'	2822'	2576'	1362'	1000'
Crystal Hut	3839'	3806'	3560'	2346'	1957'
Horstman Hut	5280'	5247'	5001'	3787'	3398'
BC Glacier	5253'	5220'	4974'	3760'	3371'

left photo: Alain Denis, bottom middle photo: Tim Smith

Rendezvous	Glacier Creek	Crystal Hut	Horstman Hut	BC Glacier
3888'	2855'	3839'	5280'	5253'
3855'	2822'	3806'	5247'	5220'
3669'	2576'	3560'	5001'	4974'
2395'	1362'	2346'	3787'	3760
2066'	1000'	1957'	3398'	3371'
0'	1033'	n/a	1392'	n/a'
1033'	0	984'	2425'	2398'
n/a	984'	0	1441'	1414'
1392	2425	1441'	0	n/a'
n/a	2398'	1414'	n/a	0

Blackcomb images clockwise from far left: enjoying the powder, Teetering Rock, skiers and riders hiking for the goods and snow rime on Horstman Hut.

Blackcomb Mountain Familiarization Tour

This is a self-guided tour for Blackcomb Mountain. It is designed to showcase the best terrain and most useful lifts for the average intermediate skier or rider. The tour will keep you on the mid to upper mountain where the conditions are more consistent.

Start at the Lightboard near the Rendezvous Restaurant (top of the Solar Coaster Express chairlift).

▷ Ski down Springboard (adjacent to Solar Chair) to the Cruiser Corner area and then on down Cruiser to Solar Load. Jump on the Solar Coaster and ride back up.

▷ Get off the Solar Coaster and ride below the Rendezvous restaurant to Wishbone (Slow Zone). Ski the top few pitches before breaking off left onto Honeycomb. Honeycomb winds itself down (crossing several other runs) and eventually ends at the Excelerator Chair. Take this chair to the top.

▷ Ski down Wishbone to the bottom of Jersey Cream Express chair. Get off the lift and head left into the large bowl. Ski Jersey Cream Run to the bottom and, this time, get on the Glacier Express Chair.

▷ Get off the Glacier Express and turn right merging onto the Horstman Glacier. Keep right and follow the Crystal Traverse to the top of Crystal Ridge Chair. Pass the top of the chair and continue straight onto Ridge Runner. Ridge Runner will eventually join the Blackcomb Glacier Road and end at the bottom of the Excelerator chair. Take this chair to the top.

▷ Get off the Excelerator chair and ski down Wishbone to upper Zig Zag. Follow Zig Zag to the bottom of the Crystal Chair and get on the lift. From the top of the Crystal Chair, head left to Rock 'N' Roll. Follow this run down to the Excelerator Chair and get on the lift.

Get off Excelerator and ski down Wishbone to the bottom of the Jersey Cream Express. Ride Jersey Cream to the top and head right off the top. Look to the left for 7th Avenue. It is above the big blue building. Ski 7th Avenue  to the bottom of 7th Heaven Express chair and load the lift.

Head right off the top of 7th Heaven Express and follow Green Road to the top of Panorama. Drop into Panorama and ride back to the bottom of 7th Heaven Express chair.

Get off 7th Heaven Express and head back down the Green Road to the top of Cloud Nine. Follow Cloud Nine back to the bottom of 7th Heaven Express.

Get off 7th Heaven Express and look for a tunnel underneath the top of the Horstman T-Bar. Ski through the tunnel onto Horstman Glacier. Cross the Horstman T-bar line (to your left) and ski Blue Line (down the middle of the glacier). Blue Line eventually becomes a cat road. The cat road will take you underneath the Crystal Chair to Zig Zag. Ski Zig Zag to the bottom of the Excelerator chair and ride to the top.

Get off the Excelerator and ski down Wishbone to the bottom of the Jersey Cream Express chair. Ride the lift up, and unload to your right. Ski down a short pitch to the Rendezvous Restaurant and the light board where you began your tour.

You have returned to the spot where you started! Now find your way back to your favorite areas and ride more of the terrain you like the best!

Magic Carpet

1. Whistler Kids . . . .
This small area located adjacent to the Blackcomb Day Lodge behind the administration building is the base area for the Kids Ski programs. It offers a small beginner slope serviced by the Magic Carpet lift (a conveyer belt). Additional photo on page 119.

Magic Chair

A slow-speed triple chair located at the base of Blackcomb that takes riders to the Base II facilities and services the beginner runs in the area.

2. YBR (Yellow Brick Road) . . . .

A short groomed run on the lower mountain from Base II to the Daylodge. YBR is one of the few fall line Green runs on Blackcomb Mountain and is the location of the "Night Moves" evening ski area. Additional photo on page 117.

3. Lower Merlins . . . .

This run under the Wizard Chair actually starts at tower six below Cruiser run and provides access to the Blackcomb Day Lodge, Chateau Whistler and condo developments adjacent to Blackcomb Mountain. Additional photo on page 117.

Tubing Centre

4. Tube Park . . . .

New for the 2005 / 2006 season is a snow tube park with something for everyone. The park offers Green, Blue and Black level tube lanes and is lit up with lights for evening sliding. The area is serviced by a 500 foot carpet lift to get maximum "tubeage" without having to hike your tube back up the hill. Conveniently, there is parking right beside the park in Lot 8 and a snack shack on site because everyone knows you can't slide without hot chocolate!

6 NIGHT PIPE

LOWER CRUISER

3

TOP OF MAGIC CHAIR

2

BASE 2

7 **4** TUBE PARK

P8

P7

12 VILLAGE RUN

P6

LOWER MERLIN'S

YELLOW BRICK ROAD

1 MAGIC CARPET

WEE WIZ HANDLE TOW TEACHING AREA

WHISTLER KIDS

BOTTOM OF MAGIC CHAIR

BOTTOM OF WIZARD EXPRESS

Blackcomb Base Overview

BASE 1

Excalibur Gondola

This gondola from Whistler Village brings guests onto Blackcomb Mountain. A commuter lift by design, "The Box" accesses a limited amount of terrain, yet is a popular ride for many young skiers. The gondola is the last point on the mountain from which you can download. With a middle station at Base II, upload is possible from the valley or upper parking lots.

5. Short Horn . . . .

Short horn is a seldom-groomed intermediate run from the top of the gondola that allows access to the good skiing on Lower Cruiser. Additional photo on page 118.

6. Lower Cruiser . . . .

A steep Blue run by most ski area standards, Lower Cruiser hosted, in 2005, the first Snowboard World Cup ever held in Canada. All this fame has caused Lower Cruiser to be well adorned with snow making capabilities. Additional photos on pages 114 and 118.

 ## Wizard Express Chair

The famous "bubble chair" from the Blackcomb Base takes you up to Midstation. Skiing below "The Wiz" can often be challenging, because snow conditions vary greatly on the lower mountain in early and late season.

7. Green Line (Midstation to Base 2) . .

The lowermost section of Green Line, also referred to as Lower Mainline, is the only novice way off Blackcomb Mountain. Initially a cat road, it splits in the lower section allowing access to both the Village (via Village Run) and Blackcomb Base (via Lower Merlin's). During the early part of the day, there is pleasant skiing for the entire length of this run, but during the afternoon rush to get off the mountain, it can be quite daunting! Additional photo on page 118.

8. Grubstake . . . .

A short run through the maze of tree islands of the lower mountain. Great pitch and daily grooming make it worth searching for. Photos on pages 118 and 130.

Lower Cruiser

SHORT HORN

MERLIN'S

GREEN LINE

SCHOOL MARM

WIZARD EXPRESS CHAIR

NIGHT PIPE

GREEN LINE

LOWER CRUISER

TOP OF MAGIC CHAIR

EXCALIBUR GONDOLA

BASE 2

TO WHISTLER VILLAGE

YBR

Wizard Express Chair

9. Merlin's

Merlin's Run is directly under the Wizard chair and can have groomed and ungroomed sections. The lower section (below tower six) is a Slow Zone. Additional photo on page 117.

10. Mainline

Mainline descends from the top of "The Wiz", initially under the chair and then far skier's left. Lower Mainline is also referred to as Green Line (see that description) and is a designated Slow Zone. Good valley views.

11. School Marm

Often used as the high-speed alternate route for skiers who want to avoid the Slow Zone at the end of the day. During the day this run offers great skiing on fun winding pitches. Additional photo on page 117.

12. Village Run

The only ski run that lets skiers return to the village from Blackcomb Mountain. Although rated Green, the run has a steeper section and often sees high traffic at the day's end. For the benefit of young skiers and the timid, downloading from Base II is likely the best option. Additional photo on page 115.

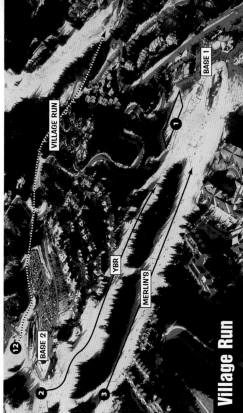

Village Run

CRUISER

24

GANDY DANCER

23

SPRINGBOARD

22

NINTENDO TERRAIN PARK

RENDEZVOUS

LIGHT BOARD

CATSKINNER BUMPS

16

19

EXPRESSWAY

TOP OF SOLAR COASTER EXPRESS

52

7TH AVENUE

53

BOTTOM OF JERSEY CREAM EXPRESS

35

35

WISHBONE

36

COUGAR MILK

TOP OF CATSKINNER CHAIR

TOP OF JERSEY CREAM EXPRESS

Solar Coaster Express Chair

The Solar Coaster is the gateway to the upper mountain and all it has to offer: restaurants, Terrain Parks, Kids Castle and skiing of all levels of difficulty.

13. Easy Out . . . .

To access Easy Out, follow Expressway towards 7th Heaven and watch for the signs. This is virtually the only area that has good beginner skiing on Blackcomb and offers access to the Children's Adventure Park and Castle. For families or novices skiing on Blackcomb, the upper portion of the run is best serviced by riding Catskinner. Additional photos on pages 125, 126 & 160.

14. Countdown & Racer Alley . . . .

Two recently cut runs accessed from Easy Out, these runs often have soft grooming long after everything else.

15. Big Easy Terrain Garden . . . .

Located below the Last Resort road, The Garden offers even the first time park rider a chance to jib. This area has rollers, banks and boxes to get your feet wet.

16. Catskinner Bumps . . . .

A great adventure for those ready to try their first Black Diamond run, this piste offers a short steep section of moguls ending with a merge onto Easy Out. Additional photos on pages 120 and 125.

17. Slingshot . . . .

Accessible from below the terrain park or the connector off Easy Out, Sling Shot is a frequently groomed cruiser with fall-away turns and a steep lower section. Photos on pages 118 and 125.

18. Lower Gearjammer . . . .

This run is a more difficult alternative to the ski-out on Blackcomb Mountain. When groomed, this is a real thigh-burning cruiser; when bumped up, it becomes essentially an easy Black run. Enjoy good views of the valley and ski-out access to the village and Blackcomb base. Photo page 118.

19. Nintendo Terrain Park . . . .

Just below the Solar Coaster Express chair off-load is the "Blackcomb Park" the intermediate spot for getting your park fix. With a massive sound system blasting fresh new vibes from the DJ shack this park offers an array of hips, boxes, rails, banks and jumps. Photos on pages 120 and 125.

Easy Out

RENDEZVOUS
RESTAURANT

51

52 53

7TH AVENUE

35 19 16

EXPRESSWAY

22

13

CATSKINNER
BUMPS

EASY OUT

LAST RESORT 54

14

15

BIG
EASY

COUNTDOWN

CHILDREN'S
ADVENTURE PARK

RACER
ALLEY

Solar Coaster Express Chair

20. Highest Level Terrain Park . . . .
Contained within the Nintendo Park is the "HL" park. This is the mother ship of terrain parks where you need a special pass and a helmet just to get in! Even the Birdman (Tony Hawk) was refused entry when he didn't have one! Go to Guest Relations and they will hook you up with what you need. The "HL" is where the sport is being pushed ever further into the future as the builders think of even more farfetched ideas for new school features. Ride Catskinner to view the action!

21. Children's Adventure Park . . . .
The Children's Adventure Park has several trails that wind and twist through the forest past a variety of interesting features, from old gold-panning cabins to railroad equipment. The final destination of all trails is the Castle, a wooden structure with slides and lookout towers staffed by special-events workers. All day long, there are activities for young skiers, and no family tour should miss a trip into the slides!

22. Springboard . . . .
One of the most popular cruising runs on Blackcomb because of its proximity to the Solar Coaster chair. Wide open for carving, Springboard sees heavy traffic by visitors getting a feel for the mountain. Additional photos on pages 120, 123, 126 and 127.

23. Gandy Dancer . . . .
Gandy is the next run north of Springboard, eventually merging with it above "Cruiser Corner." This run offers great carving with several natural rollers thrown in for fun. Gandy is a popular training ground for young racers and is often the site of regional, national and international races. Much less traffic than Springboard. Additional photos on pages 120, 126 and 127.

24. Cruiser . . . .
Cruiser run is accessed via Wishbone from the top of Solar Coaster Express (upper Wishbone is a SLOW ZONE). This slope has fantastic "cruising", but it's tricky not getting lost as you crisscross several other runs. Cruiser is a long run split into two sections; Lower Cruiser is the name of the run once you cross Green Line below Excalibur. Additional photos on pages 118, 120, 126, 127, 128, 129, 130 & 131.

25. Cruiser Corner . . . .
This is the name of the flat "rest area" where Springboard, Gandy Dancer, and Cruiser all intersect. This is a good spot to stop and collect your group and plan the last pitch to ski to the bottom of Solar Coaster. Photo on page 127.

Catskinner

TOP OF CATSKINNER CHAIR

51

53

52

TOP OF SOLAR COASTER EXPRESS

RENDEZVOUS RESTAURANT

35

16

WISHBONE

23

22

24

CRUISER

EASY OUT

29

NINTENDO TERRAIN PARK

HIGHEST LEVEL

ADVENTURE PARK

21

21

19

20

13

GANDY DANCER

17

28

SRPINGBOARD

SLINGSHOT

Solar Coaster Express Chair

26. Cruiser / Stoker Bumps . . . .
These two short sections of mogul skiing can be found off the Cruiser Run. Additional photo on page 129.

27. Stoker . . . .
Seldom-groomed Stoker is a lower-angled run that is an often forgotten gem on powder days. Additional photos on pages 118 and 130.

28. Green Line (Catskinner Load to Cruiser Corner) . .
This section of road has been left off the mountain map in recent years to discourage beginners from venturing in this direction. This road crosses several high speed runs and the exit from the terrain park and slow riders can feel like the ducks in a shooting gallery game. Best avoided unless there is no other option open. Additional photo on page 125.

29. Jersey Cream Road . . . .
JCR is a strange novice track that starts in the middle of a Blue run. Originally, it linked the top of the Stoker Chair with Jersey Cream Chair to access the alpine. Stoker was removed in the early 90's and now JCR is simply a convenient traverse to Jersey Cream and Glacier Express chairs. Additional photos on pages 125 and 128.

Cruiser

TOP OF SOLAR COASTER EXPRESS

24

29 23 22

26 SRPINGBOARD

CRUISER
BUMPS

26

STOKER
BUMPS

GANDY
DANCER

28

25

30

24 27

STOKER

CRUISER

Blackcomb Mountain

CRUISER

TOP OF EXCELERATOR EXPRESS

ACCESS TO JCR & HONEYCOMB

29

24

31

33

32

HONEYCOMB

ESPRESSO

BUZZ CUT

Excelerator Express Chair

"Excel" is the quad chair that continues the trip to the alpine from the gondola. Situated at mid-mountain, Excel offers access to predominantly intermediate skiing on wide cruising runs. It is also the lift that returns skiers to the upper mountain runs that come out of the Blackcomb Glacier after 11 km of skiing! Continue up from Excel via a short ski to the Jersey Cream Express.

30. Green Line (Jersey Cream to Midstation)

Also known as Solar Coaster Road, Green Line is the only novice ski out from the Jersey Cream base area. From the flats beside Glacier Creek restaurant (top of Zig Zag), this road crosses the runs on skiers' left. Follow it all the way down to Midstation (Wizard unload / Solar Coaster load) or the Excelerator load. Additionally, Green Line may be accessed via Jersey Cream Road from the Excel unload station. Additional photos on pages 126, 127, 130 and 131.

31. Honeycomb

Accessible either from Wishbone or the top of Excelerator Chair, Honeycomb is another fantastic cruising run that has big elbow bends, rollers, and fall-away pitches. Similar to Cruiser, the run can be confusing the first few times because it crosses several other similar runs, take it slow the first time and watch for signs until you figure out where the run goes. Additional photos on pages 130, 131 and 134.

32. Buzzcut

A short Blue run off the top of Excelerator Chair that eventually merges with Honeycomb. More photos on pages 131 and 134.

Green Line

TOP OF EXCELERATOR EXPRESS

ESPRESSO
HONEY-COMB
GREEN LINE
CRUISER

Excelerator Express Chair

33. Espresso . . . .

The name of the run under the Excelerator chair. Watch out for open creeks, as there is a warm spring that flows along the run. Additional photos on pages 128 and 129.

34. Zig Zag . . . .

Zig Zag is a fantastic cruising run and immensely popular especially early in the day when linked up with Wishbone. Traffic builds up during ski out, as Zig Zag is a commuter run for all the skiing in Jersey Cream and the Crystal Ridge. Additional photos on pages 136 and 137.

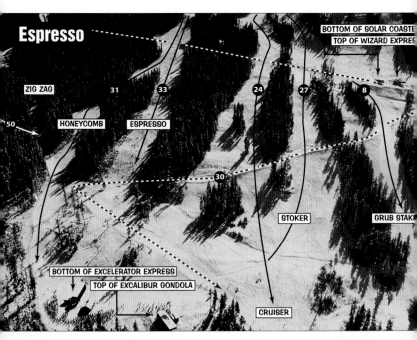

Espresso

BOTTOM OF SOLAR COASTE
TOP OF WIZARD EXPRES

ZIG ZAG   31   33   24   27   8
50
HONEYCOMB   ESPRESSO
30
STOKER   GRUB STAK
BOTTOM OF EXCELERATOR EXPRESS
TOP OF EXCALIBUR GONDOLA
CRUISER

Espresso

TOP OF EXCELERATOR EXPRESS

BUZZ CUT

32 33 31

34 30

GREEN LINE

24

ZIG ZAG

HONEYCOMB

50

RESCUE ROAD

ESPRESSO

CRUISER

30

BOTTOM OF EXCELERATOR EXPRESS

TOP OF EXCALIBUR GONDOLA

131

CRYSTAL TRAVERSE

45

46

HEAVENLY BASIN

BLUE LINE

GLACIER DRIVE

JERSEY CREAM EXPRESS CHAIR

GLACIER EXPRESS CHAIR

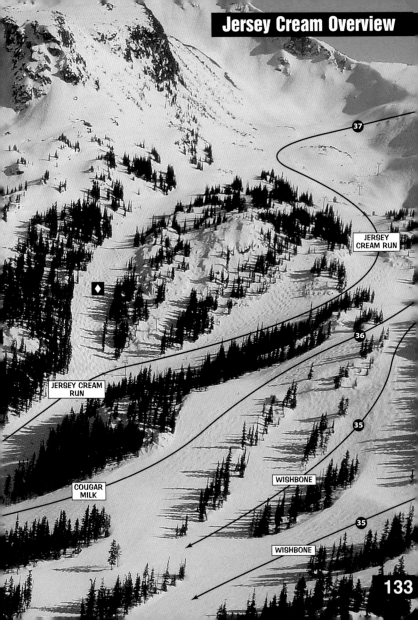

Jersey Cream Overview

37

JERSEY
CREAM RUN

◆

JERSEY CREAM
RUN

36

35

COUGAR
MILK

WISHBONE

35

WISHBONE

133

Jersey Cream Express Chair

"JC" is one of the more popular chairs on the mountain. It offers access to great intermediate runs that stretch from tree line to a mid mountain plateau and large restaurant Glacier Creek. At 1500 feet, the snow quality stays great, and the spring skiing is unbeatable.

35. Wishbone . . . .

Quite possibly the busiest run in the alpine on Blackcomb, Wishbone is a designated Slow Zone. The Mountain Safety Team and Ski Patrol police this run to calm traffic and provide an intermediate slope for those learning to ski and snowboard. More photos on pages 121, 123, 125 and 133.

36. Cougar Milk . . . .

This run is pinched between Wishbone and the Jersey Cream chair. It offers more quality cruising with a slightly steeper pitch than Wishbone and much less traffic. More photos pages 121 and 133.

37. Jersey Cream . . . .

This cruiser descends from the top of the Jersey Cream chair into the bottom of Jersey Cream Bowl, allowing great views up into the Double Black Diamond terrain of the Couloir Extreme. Additional photo on page 133.

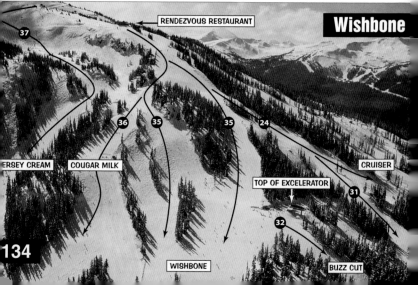

RENDEZVOUS RESTAURANT

Wishbone

37

36 35 35 24

JERSEY CREAM COUGAR MILK CRUISER

TOP OF EXCELERATOR

31

32

WISHBONE BUZZ CUT

Jersey Cream

TOP OF JERSEY CREAM EXPRESS

RENDEZVOUS RESTAURANT

35

35

37

36

COUGAR MILK

JERSEY CREAM

BOTTOM OF GLACIER EXPRESS

BOTTOM OF JERSEY CREAM EXPRESS

GLACIER CREEK LODGE

135

Blackcomb Mountain

Crystal Chair

Crystal Ridge is serviced by this old-style fixed-grip triple chair, which makes the area feel like a little ski hill within a big ski area. This self-contained part of the resort has its own quaint restaurant (serves great waffles!) and offers some of the best and quietest skiing on either mountain. Although limited to only one novice run, the area has fantastic intermediate cruisers and would be the perfect spot for a solid beginner to step it up to the intermediate level. Don't miss this area!

38. Crystal Road ....

Of all the Green roads on Blackcomb, Crystal Road is the most pleasant. It offers tranquil, winding skiing from the top of Crystal Chair down to Glacier Creek / Jersey Cream bowl. Choose between continuing along Green Line or returning to Crystal Chair load. Additional photo on page 139.

39. Trapline ....

A shorter Blue run descending from the Crystal Road to the bottom of Crystal Chair, groomed on an alternating basis with White Light. Additional photo on page139.

40. White Light ....

This enjoyable intermediate run intersects the Blue Line switchback below Crystal Chair, and continues down the skiers left of the chairlift to the bottom.

41. Rock 'N' Roll ....

One of several super-cruisers in this area, these runs have great flow, low traffic volume and few confusing interconnecting runs. All of the runs in this area can be cut short to stay on the Crystal Chair, or for full value, ski top to bottom and ride the Excelerator chair to get back to the Crystal Ridge. Additional photos on pages 138 and 139.

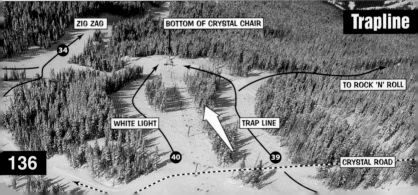

ZIG ZAG

BOTTOM OF CRYSTAL CHAIR

Trapline

34

TO ROCK 'N' ROLL

WHITE LIGHT

TRAP LINE

40

39

CRYSTAL ROAD

Trapline

CRYSTAL HUT

TOP OF CRYSTAL CHAIR

CRYSTAL TRAVERSE

45

38

39

BLUE LINE

46

41

40

ROCK 'N' ROLL

BOTTOM OF GLACIER EXPRESS

GLACIER CREEK RESTAURANT

38

39

40

34

TRAP LINE

WHITE LIGHT

TO LOWER ROCK 'N' ROLL

ZIG ZAG

BOTTOM OF CRYSTAL CHAIR

137

Blackcomb Mountain

42. Backstage Pass . . . .

Backstage Pass is an off-fall-line run cut from Rock 'N' Roll crossing over past Ridge Runner to the Blackcomb Glacier Rescue Road. It is groomed on an infrequent basis all or in part.

43. Ridge Runner . . . .

Possibly the best Blue run at Whistler Blackcomb— if not the world! Ridge Runner offers amazing carving on a winding run with fun corners, banks and steep pitches. Do not miss a trip (or 10) down this run! Additional photo on page 154.

44. Twist and Shout . . . .

Groomed on an alternating basis with Rock' N' Roll and Backstage Pass, Twist and Shout is another super fun carving run with undulating terrain and a natural half-pipe feature. If it has recently been groomed, it is a contender for the most fun you can have on skis! Additional photo on page 154.

Ridge Runner

44

43

42

41

ROCK 'N' ROLL

RESCUE ROAD

BACKSTAGE PASS

RIDGE RUNNER

50

Ridge Runner

CRYSTAL TRAVERSE

CRYSTAL HUT

TOP OF CRYSTAL CHAIR

45

46

38

39

CRYSTAL ROAD

BLUE LINE

41

TRAP LINE

38

44

43

42

TWIST & SHOUT

ROCK 'N' ROLL

RIDGE RUNNER

BACKSTAGE PASS

139

Glacier Express Chair

"GE" is the high-speed quad that takes skiers up to the North Side high alpine and skiing on the Horstman Glacier. There is **no** "easy way out" from the top of GE! There is an intermediate run that traverses to Crystal Ridge and some good intermediate skiing on the Glacier. During bad storms, GE may be the highest lift open on the mountain. In these conditions, strong intermediate skiers can still access the *middle* section of Blue Line and Crystal Traverse using GE.

45. Crystal Traverse . . . .
Crystal Traverse begins at the top of the 7th Heaven chair and crosses the Horstman Glacier, eventually crossing under the Glacier Express chair to wind its way to the top of Crystal Chair and the Crystal Hut. Watch for rocks on the Hot Rocks section above Heavenly Basin. Additional photos on pages 132, 137, 139, 142, 144, 145, 147 and 156.

46. Blue Line . . . .
The best intermediate run on the north side, this thigh burner starts behind the Horstman Hut at the top of 7th Heaven and runs down the glacier all the way to the Glacier Creek restaurant. The bottom section becomes a cat road, but many people opt to take Glacier Drive (advanced - see page 132) to keep skiing fall line. More photos on pages 132, 137, 139, 143, 144, 145, and 147.

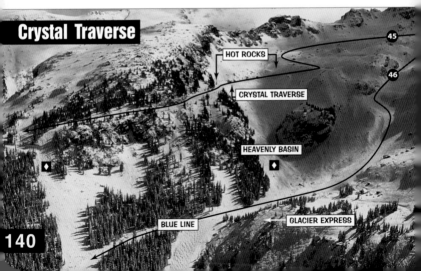

Crystal Traverse

45

46

HOT ROCKS

CRYSTAL TRAVERSE

HEAVENLY BASIN

BLUE LINE

GLACIER EXPRESS

Blue Line

TOP OF GLACIER EXPRESS

CRYSTAL TRAVERSE

48

45

46

◆

GLACIER EXPRESS

BLUE LINE

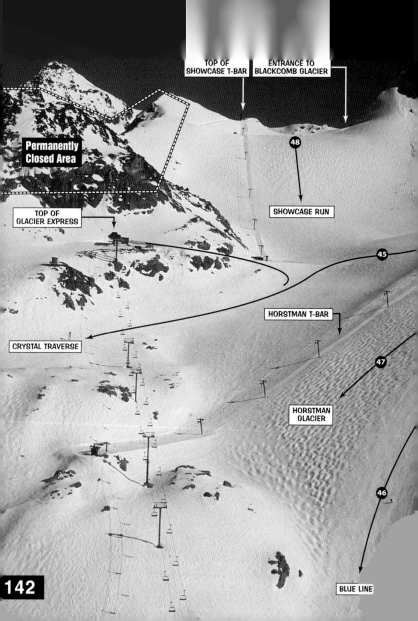

TOP OF
SHOWCASE T-BAR

ENTRANCE TO
BLACKCOMB GLACIER

**Permanently
Closed Area**

TOP OF
GLACIER EXPRESS

SHOWCASE RUN

CRYSTAL TRAVERSE

HORSTMAN T-BAR

HORSTMAN
GLACIER

BLUE LINE

142

TOP OF
HORSTMAN T-BAR

TOP OF 7TH
HEAVEN EXPRESS

HORSTMAN HUT

45

47

46

♦

Horstman T-Bar

This surface lift allows skiers on the north side to ride up to the top of the 7th Heaven area and ski the sunny runs on the south side, or traverse back to the Rendezvous Restaurant. This is a steep T-bar and may not be great for first time T-bar riders because of the extremely steep pitch at the top!

47. Horstman Glacier . . . .

The Horstman Glacier is the longest lasting ski run in North America. This slope is open for skiing from November to August every year! Additional photos on pages 143 and 147.

Horstman Unload

TOP OF 7TH HEAVEN EXPRESS

TOP OF HORSTMAN T-BAR

HORSTMAN HUT

VIEWPOINT

45

46

47

BLUE LINE

HORSTMAN GLACIER

CRYSTAL TRAVERSE

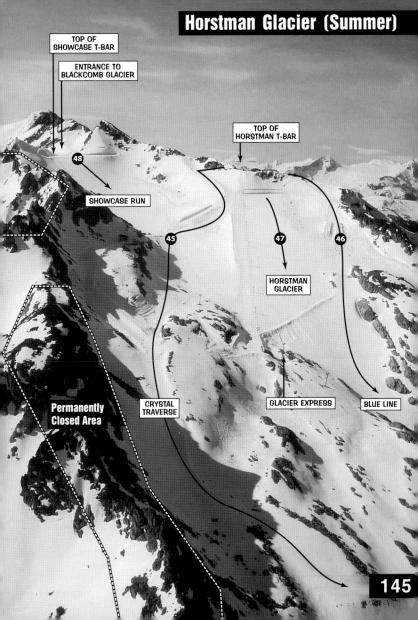

TOP OF
SHOWCASE T-BAR

ENTRANCE TO
BLACKCOMB GLACIER

TOP OF
HORSTMAN T-BAR

48

SHOWCASE RUN

45

47

46

HORSTMAN
GLACIER

Permanently
Closed Area

CRYSTAL
TRAVERSE

GLACIER EXPRESS

BLUE LINE

Showcase T-Bar

The uppermost lift on either mountain takes you to 7400 feet above sea level! Showcase is the lift that gains skiers access to the Blackcomb Glacier Provincial Park and its amazing views! No Green runs up here!

48. Showcase Run . . . .

The Showcase Run parallels the T-bar of the same name. If cruising is your thing stick to the groomed passes; if powder is more your style, try the skier's right side of the T-bar. Additional photos on pages 141, 142 and 145.

ENTRANCE TO BLACKCOMB GLACIER

BLOW HOLE

BOOTPACK UP TO BLACKCOMB GLACIER

AVALANCHE SIGN

Blackcomb Glacier Provincial Pa

☐ This area is for intermediates and experts o
◇ There is no grooming on the top section.
◆ Be aware, conditions vary greatly day to da

BC Parks

BLACKCOMB GLACIER

Avalanche Prone Area

CLOSED

HORSTMAN PEAK

TOP OF SHOWCASE T-BAR

ENTRANCE TO BLACKCOMB GLACIER

Permanently Closed Area

48

SHOWCASE RUN

CRYSTAL TRAVERSE

TOP OF GLACIER EXPRESS

45

47

HORSTMAN T-BAR

HORSTMAN GLACIER

46

BLUE LINE

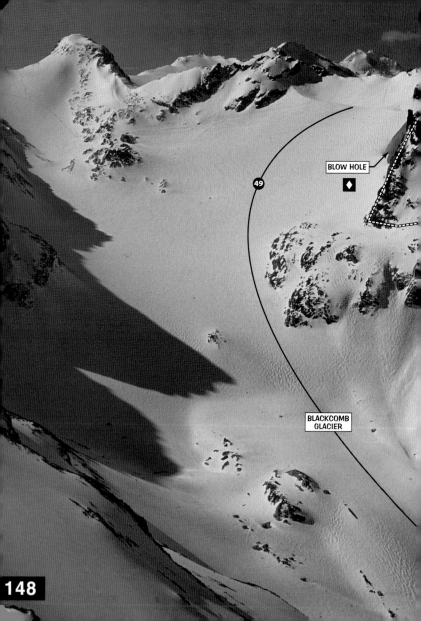

BLOW HOLE ♦

49

BLACKCOMB GLACIER

TOP OF
HOWCASE T-BAR

HORSTMAN
GLACIER

**Permanently
Closed Area**

BLACKCOMB
GLACIER

49

FLAT AREA

SWAMP THING

50

TOP OF SHOWCASE T-BAR &
BLACKCOMB GLACIER ENTRANCE

**Permanently
Closed Area**

50

RESCUE ROAD

151

49. Blackcomb Glacier . . . .

. . . .

This run gets five stars out of three— an amazing 13 kilometers of skiing before you need to ride another chairlift! This run passes through the Blackcomb Glacier Provincial Park, which is avalanche controlled by Blackcomb Ski Patrol. Incredible views of the Double Black Diamond bowls and nearby backcountry are afforded all along the way. Although given the Blue rating, this could be the world's hardest Blue run, so make sure your group contains confident intermediate skiers and snowboarders. Additional photos on pages 148, 150 and 155.

Blackcomb Glacier

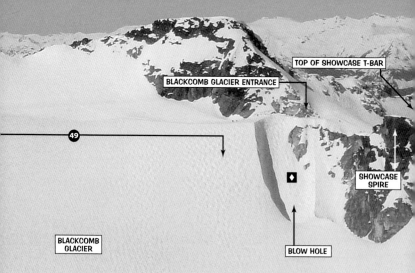

TOP OF SHOWCASE T-BAR

BLACKCOMB GLACIER ENTRANCE

49

SHOWCASE SPIRE

BLOW HOLE

BLACKCOMB GLACIER

50. Rescue Road

The cat road out of the back bowls, Blackcomb Glacier Rescue Road traverses from the bottom of the glacier to the Excelerator chair. The drop-in point for the road is at the end of Swamp Thing where the information board and rest stop are located. The road can feel like the Autobahn, an intimidating experience for young guests or beginners, so time your descent with a lull in activity for the best experience. Additional photos on pages 108, 118, 130, 131, 138 and 151.

Rescue Road

RESCUE ROAD

43

44

50

TWIST & SHOUT

TO EXCELERATOR
EXPRESS CHAIR

BLACKCOMB GLACIER

49

SWAMP THING

50

Permanently Closed Area

RESCUE ROAD

TO EXCELERATOR EXPRESS

Blackcomb Mountain

7th Heaven Express Chair

On a sunny day this is the place to be. The views in every direction are incredible! 7th Heaven is the highest point on the mountain where skiers can take a Green run all the way to the Valley. Horstman Hut offers food and washrooms, if needed.

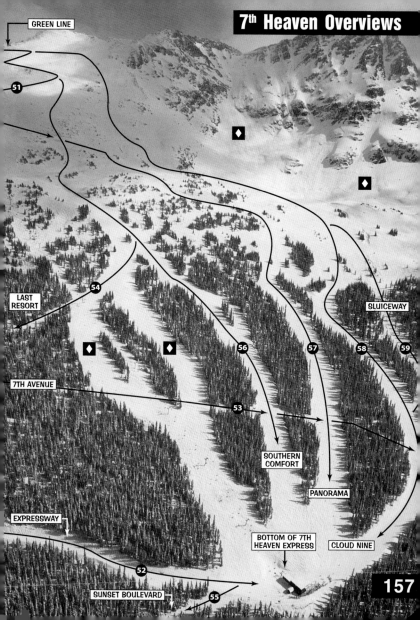

GREEN LINE

51

LAST
RESORT

54

SLUICEWAY

7TH AVENUE

56   57   58   59

53

SOUTHERN
COMFORT

PANORAMA

EXPRESSWAY

BOTTOM OF 7TH
HEAVEN EXPRESS

CLOUD NINE

52

SUNSET BOULEVARD   55

7th Heaven Express Chair

51. Green Line . . . .

Green Line winds its way down the south side of 7th Heaven, traversing around the mountain to the Rendezvous Restaurant. Additional photos on pages 123, 125, 156, 157, 160, 161 and 162.

Green Line

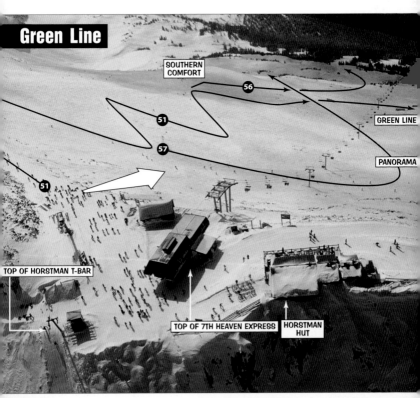

SOUTHERN COMFORT

56

51

GREEN LINE

57

PANORAMA

51

TOP OF HORSTMAN T-BAR

TOP OF 7TH HEAVEN EXPRESS

HORSTMAN HUT

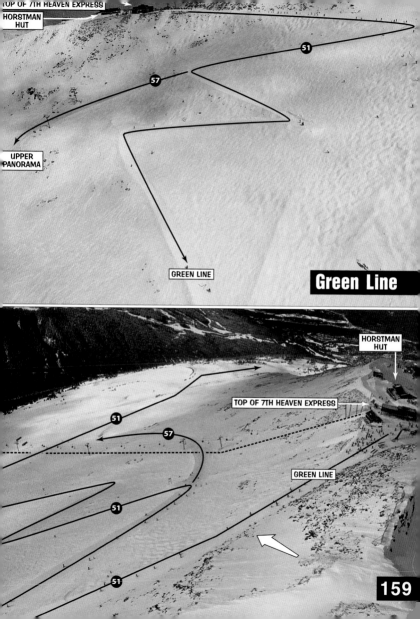

TOP OF 7TH HEAVEN EXPRESS

HORSTMAN HUT

51

57

UPPER PANORAMA

GREEN LINE

Green Line

HORSTMAN HUT

TOP OF 7TH HEAVEN EXPRESS

51

57

GREEN LINE

51

51

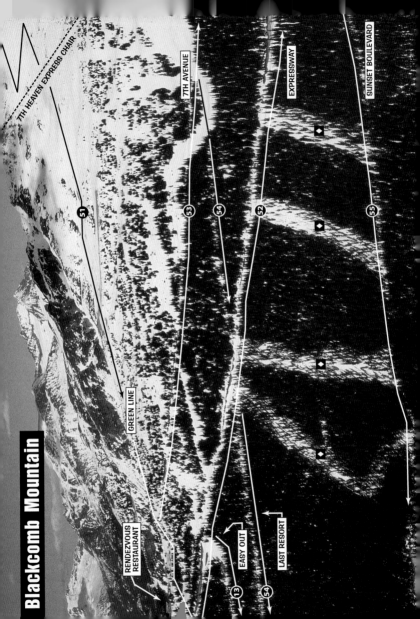

Blackcomb Mountain

7TH HEAVEN EXPRESS CHAIR

7TH AVENUE

EXPRESSWAY

SUNSET BOULEVARD

GREEN LINE

RENDEZVOUS RESTAURANT

EASY OUT

LAST RESORT

51

53

54

52

55

13

54

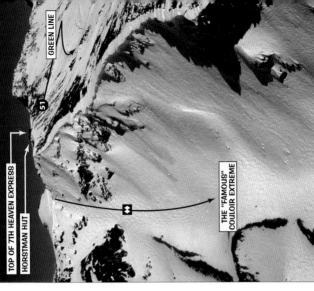

TOP OF 7TH HEAVEN EXPRESS
HORSTMAN HUT

GREEN LINE

51

THE "FAMOUS" COULOIR EXTREME

52. Expressway

Expressway is the cat road that links the Rendezvous Restaurant area with the base of the 7th Heaven Express Chair. Additional photos on pages 120, 123, 125, 156 and 157.

53. 7th Avenue

7th Ave. is accessible from the top of Jersey Cream and Catskinner chairs, or as an extension of the Green Line returning skiers to the bottom of 7th Heaven chair. Although technically a Green run (read road), this run eventually spits riders out onto the final section of a Blue run. Additional photos on pages 120, 123, 125, 157 and 163.

54. Last Resort

Last Resort is a strange cat road that starts seemingly nowhere. It is best accessed from 7th Avenue and used to return skiers to the runs on the front side of the mountain, as it merges with Easy Out. Additional photos on pages 123, 157, 162 and 163.

55. Sunset Boulevard

Sunset is the cat road from the bottom of 7th Heaven that returns skiers to the top of the Wizard chair on the front side. At the end of the day it can have high traffic, as it is the only egress from the south side. Beginner riders are advised to avoid this run at the end of the day if possible. Additional photos on pages 109, 156 and 157.

7th Heaven Express Chair

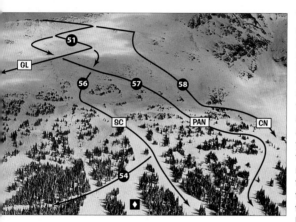

These final descriptions are for the ultra-popular intermediate runs on the south side of 7th Heaven. The upper section often causes some confusion about where one run starts and the other ends above tree line. Once you are into the trees, the runs each become much clearer. Follow the large posted signs that indicate the runs at the top of the Green Line traverse.

56. Southern Comfort ....

Southern Comfort sees less grooming then the other runs because of the natural terrain features. As a result, it can form moguls when the others don't. Don't let that deter you from skiing this exceptional run. Additional photos on pages 157 and 158.

57. Panorama ....

Panorama offers fantastic cruising on several fun, steeper pitches with natural rest stops for those who need them. Additional photos on pages 156, 157, 158 and 159.

58. Cloud Nine ....

The skier's leftmost line on the south side before you enter the Black Diamond Xhiggy's Meadow, Cloud Nine offers the best view up into the massive Lakeside Bowl. Views matched with fantastic high-alpine cruising make this a candidate for the best run of this level on either mountain. Additional photo on page 157.

59. Sluiceway ....

Sluiceway is a short run that breaks off left from Cloud Nine at the tree line. It is characterized by natural rolls and bumps and does not see any grooming. Photo on page 157.

7TH HEAVEN
EXPRESS

LAST
RESORT

54

56

57

58

53

SOUTHERN
COMFORT

PANORAMA

7TH AVENUE

CLOUD
NINE

BOTTOM OF 7TH HEAVEN EXPRESS

Skiing & Snowboarding With Children

Ski / Snowboard School for Children:

The ski / snowboard school for children is called Whistler Kids and promises "memories and learning … through encouragement, accomplishment and friendship". Parents interested in signing their children up for Whistler Kids programs can do so at several locations. They have facilities in the Creekside and Village that access Whistler Mountain and Blackcomb Base and Base II for programs on Blackcomb Mountain. All locations offer convenient drop-off areas to ease the process of getting kids and gear from car to door.

Whistler Kids offers six levels of instruction with specific goals for each level to help your child progress as a skier or snowboarder. The goals for each level are as follows;

- **Level 1:** Skiing- To turn both ways and stop. Snowboarding- To have good directional control while side slipping and traversing.

- **Level 2:** Skiing- To match the skis parallel at the end of the turn on Green terrain. Snowboarding- To link turns on Green terrain.

- **Level 3**: Skiing- Ski with a wide parallel stance and learn to pole plant. Snowboarding- Able to vary turn shape and adapt to uneven terrain.

- **Level 4:** Skiing- Strong parallel turns on Blue runs, easier Black runs and in a variety of snow conditions. Snowboarding- To ride confidently on Blue runs and in a variety of conditions.

- **Level 5:** Skiing- Improve edging and timing & coordination on varied terrain and conditions. Snowboarding- Improve pressure control and timing & coordination.

- **Level 6:** Skiing & Snowboarding- Continue to refine all skills in varied terrain and snow conditions.

Terrain Parks:

Whistler and Blackcomb have dedicated areas with freestyle features like jumps, banks and jibs that are designated as Terrain Parks. The idea behind the terrain park is to allow jumping in a controlled environment. All parks are fenced off with an obvious entrance. The size of the features in the park are clearly marked both at the top of the park and on each successive stunt. Park users are strongly encouraged to wear helmets and protective equipment (wrist guards) when doing freestyle maneuvers as the risk of injury increases when freestyle moves are being attempted.

A few tips for parents accompanying kids in the Terrain Parks:

- ⊤ Small and Medium Features – kids should be minimum Level 4 ability.

- ⊤ Medium Features & Halfpipe – kids should be minimum Level 5 ability.

- ⊤ Super Pipe and Large Features – kids should be solid experts.

- ⊤ Stop at the Park entrance and read the rules sign with your children.

- ⊤ Slide through the Park and scout all the features before attempting any.

- ⊤ Ensure someone in the group "spots" the jumps to ensure a clear landing zone.

- ⊤ Clear landing zone immediately and wait in a safe area.

- ⊤ Avoid the Park when overly busy.

Skiing & Snowboarding With Children

🏞️ Kid's Adventure Zones:

The Blackcomb Adventure Park is located off the run Easy Out. Look for it on the skier's left side of the run. For multiple trips through the area use the Catskinner Chairlift. This area features a number of trails that wind through the forest past attractions like a gold miner cabin, mining equipment and a railroad tunnel. The trails are of varying difficulties with archway entrances off Easy Out. All eventually end at The Castle. Which is a large structure with bridges, stairs, slides and secret passage ways for kids of all ages to explore.

The Adventure Park is monitored and maintained by a crew of Whistler Kid's employees and there is always a staff member at the castle with a radio in case of emergencies. The staff also adds animation to the area with music, theme days and activities for little visitors. The Green entrance and exit from the park will require a minimum Level 3 ability while the Blue and Black entrances and exits will require a minimum Level 4. It is possible to walk directly in to the Castle via a short trail 250m uphill from the bottom of the Catskinner Chair if there are kids in your group that cannot manages the ski in.

The Whistler Treefort is located off the run Bear Cub on the skier's right hand side of the run. Enter the area through the tunnel and rack your equipment on the stands provided. The Treefort has several elevated houses connected by bridges, winding stair cases and slides. The setting high in the coastal rainforest makes the area feel like a set from the Ewok planet in Star Wars! The Treefort staff will often have games, music and skills challenges for kids and parents lucky enough to find the area. Don't miss this attraction it is well worth the trip!

Children's Learning Center:

The Children's Learning Center (CLC) is a beautiful lodge dedicated exclusively to kids and is visible on the right as you leave from

Olympic Station on the upper line of the Whistler Village Gondola. It is the on-mountain base of operations for the Whistler Kids program and is equipped with its own kitchen, dining area and play rooms.

The adjacent, corralled "learn to ski" area is serviced by its own carpet tow lift as well as a handle tow. There are enough activities here to exhaust even the most energetic little skiers, with foam blocks, slalom gates, limbo flags and even little jumps.

The Treefort on Whistler Mountain.

167

Injured or Missing Kids:

The Ski Patrol is trained and experienced in dealing with injured or missing persons.

In the event of an <u>injury</u>:

- ☐ Secure the scene by crossing skis above the child.
- ☐ Send for patrol with information on your exact location.
- ☐ Keep child warm.
- ☐ Assist Patrol with medical history of child.

In the event of a child becoming <u>separated</u> from your group:

- ☐ Search the immediate area, leave one party member at the bottom of the most likely run.
- ☐ Notify Patrol on mountain phones (Whistler 5300, Blackcomb 7602) and inform them as to the following:
  - Where was the last seen point?
  - What was the child wearing?
  - What is the child's ability?
  - How well do they know the mountain?
- ☐ Maintain contact with the Patrol
  - Provide the Ski Patrol with both cell phone numbers and local phone number where you can be reached.

- Keep skiing the same area where you last saw the child and wait for instructions.

- Notify patrol or dispatch if you locate your child without their assistance.

All children should carry an info card in their jacket along with a whistle. The info card should have child's name, local address, medical concerns, a list of their equipment and phone numbers for multiple adults familiar with the child. Teach your children to use the whistle and wave down an adult to assist them.

Members of the Whistler Blackcomb Ski Patrol.

How They Do It

Ever wonder how the mountain ends up every morning with a fresh surface of "corduroy"? What about how there can be skiing to the valley when the golf courses down the road are open? These seemingly impossible situations are the result of hard work of the talented grooming and snowmaking crews at Whistler Blackcomb.

Grooming:

Every night, 15 to 20 snow cat operators work through the darkness to plow and shape more than 300 acres of terrain. Here is a look at the machines they use:

Snow Cats:

Snow cats are the backbone of the grooming operation and are able to groom slopes as steep as 35 degrees. These machines are equipped with a snowplow blade on the front and tiller on the back. The blade allows the driver to scoop and push snow over obstacles to ensure an even distribution of snow on the ski run. The tiller is a mechanical device that grinds up the surface of the snow, softening the top layer and forming it into the fresh corduroy pattern familiar to skiers and snowboarders.

Winch Cats:

Winch cats can be considered souped-up versions of the regular snow cat. Each machine has a massive cable winch attached to a swiveling arm. The winch cat is specifically designed to groom slopes that are too steep to climb in a regular machine (up to 75 degrees!). The operator attaches the vehicle to an anchor at the top

Snow Cat

of the slope, and uses the winch to help raise and lower the machine down steep pitches while performing the additional tasks of grooming the slope. Winch cats are used on seemingly moderate pitches like Upper Franz's, as well as on crazy steeps like Shale Slope and the Couloir Extreme.

Park Cats:

Park cats are the evolution of the snow cats and are specifically designed for building the myriad of jumps and jibs found in the terrain parks. Special blades and skilled drivers allow for this creation. The Zaug or Pipe Dragon is a special front-mounted tiller that allows the drivers to grind and shape the snow into the perfect transitions of the half-pipes.

Dump Cats:

A newer monster cat in the fleet, the dump cat is a hybrid mix of dump truck and snow cat that allows for snow to be transported from areas of abundance high up on the mountain to areas that may need a patch-up. They are often used to maintain the runs on the lower mountain.

Bun Wagons:

The bun wagons are snow cats with huge cargo boxes used to transport everything you eat, drink and blow your nose on while up on the mountain. Bun wagons run up and down all night stocking the shelves, but they are not equipped with the tools to groom the snow.

Park Cat

How They Do It

Snowmaking:

Snowmaking at Whistler Blackcomb is truly an art form. Although the Whistler Valley can receive in excess of 30 feet of snow over the winter, adequate coverage can be an issue, especially on the lower slopes. Consider the fact that it is not unheard of for the valley temperatures in Whistler to range from minus 30 degrees Celsius to plus 15 degrees Celsius throughout the season. Throw in the odd winter rainstorm, and the challenge of maintaining good ski conditions becomes apparent. Thankfully, the capacity for making snow at Whistler Blackcomb is staggering. If the conditions are right, the snowmakers can produce 40 acre feet (a unique unit of measurement used in the snowmaking industry) of snow in 24 hours. That's enough to cover an entire football field with 40 feet of snow!

photo: Tim Smit

Sometimes you have to make your own weather. Snowmaking on Blackcomb (foreground) and Whistler (across the valley).

Snowmaking machines have evolved over the years from simple sprinkler units that mixed compressed air with water to high-tech machines equipped with sensors that detect the right conditions and automatically kick into action.

In certain conditions, a chemical is added to the mix of air and water in order to create snow. Snowmax is an inert bacterium that allows water to form into snow at warmer temperatures. A naturally occurring bacterium that was discovered in Florida (of all places), Snowmax forms the nucleus around which the water droplets freeze into snow.

Snow Guns:

Whistler Blackcomb currently has 160 snow guns, with more on the shopping list for the years leading up to the Olympics. The mountains use a mix of several types of guns in specific areas to achieve their snowmaking goals. Snow guns are portable units on wheels that can be moved from area to area and are connected to hydrants. The areas equipped with hydrants are the highest-traffic ski runs, the lower-mountain ski outs, and the terrain parks.

Towers:

Gun towers are elevated structures that are capable of distributing massive amounts of snow over a larger area than the surface-based snow guns. By spreading out the man-made snow as soon as it is produced, a more natural coverage (requiring less machine work) is created.

Reservoirs:

Of course, all the snowmaking equipment in the world could not create a single crystal of snow if there was no water supply. Whistler Blackcomb has three large reservoirs that hold more than 42 million gallons of water. This amount can allow for continuous snowmaking at full capacity for four days.

About the Authors

Brian Finestone is employed year-round as the Public Safety Supervisor for Whistler and Blackcomb Mountains. He has dedicated over ten years to providing rescue services in the mountains, working in Canada and abroad as a professional ski patroller, avalanche forecaster and avalanche rescue dog handler.

A self-described "alpine generalist", Brian is equally at home on alpine skis,

snowboard, telemark skis or with a pair of ice axes in hand. His passion for winter mountain sports can only be eclipsed by his passion for rock climbing in any of its different forms.

Brian resides in Whistler with his wife, son and avalanche rescue dog.

Acknowledgments

The creation of a book usually involves many more people than those who receive credit on the front cover. This publication is certainly no exception. Several talented people were involved in this project and we would like to thank the following:

Marc Bourdon for sticking with us and, once again, helping us create a product of exceptional quality. Ian Hodder for editing volumes of our rambling text. Joe Lammers, Luis Pascal, Sonja Flepp and Jun Yanagisawa for their translating services. Damian Cromwell for his aerial lens work on short notice. Tim Smith and Joe Hertz for access to their well-documented archive of mountain photography. Insight Photography for supporting our project with visually inspiring action and scenic photography.

Kevin Hodder splits his time between guiding in the mountains and working as a television producer. He is certified by the Association of Canadian Mountain Guides as a Rock-Climbing Guide, Assistant Alpine-Climbing Guide and an Assistant Ski Guide.

Kevin has long served as the Race Manger for the Eco-Challenge expedition race, which has taken him to such locales as Australia, Morocco, Argentina, Malaysia, New Zealand and Fiji. His work can also be seen on the popular television series "Survivor" (CBS) and "Treasure Hunters"

(NBC) where he is a member of the team responsible for producing the challenges.

Kevin has climbed and skied at several international locations and maintains a boyish enthusiasm for both. To facilitate his schedule, Kevin resides with his wife Meredith, in both Whistler and Santa Monica, California.

Whistler Blackcomb and its Senior Leadership Team for endorsing our idea and supporting the project. Brian Leighton and Robert Kennedy for their invaluable advice and words of encouragement.

A final thanks goes to our families. Abbie and Finn Finestone and Meredith Rozbitsky for tolerating the piles of paper and boxes of books in the house. And, of course, our parents for teaching us that anything is possible if you put your mind to it (and for taking us skiing!).

You have all made a large impact on this book and we sincerely appreciate it!

Glossary

Advanced:
A term used to describe someone capable of skiing or snowboarding Black Diamond terrain.

Alpine:
A term used to describe the portion of the mountain above the "tree line".

Avalanche:
Massive amounts of snow sliding down hill gathering momentum and force as it travels.

Backcountry:
The fabled land beyond the boundary ropes where the only rules are the laws of nature.

Beginner:
A skier or snowboarder learning to master the skills required to successfully slide down a Green run without falling.

Cat Track:
A ski run, the width of a single lane road. Cat tracks are used by snowcats, snowmobiles and skiers alike.

Carpet Tow:
A conveyer belt used to transport beginner skiers up hill. An evolutionary leap from the dreaded rope tow.

Commuter Route:
A ski run or cat track used to get to and from parts of the mountain. Often narrow and congested, these runs are best to be used for this purpose only and not for practicing your turns.

Corduroy:
No not the pants you wore in elementary school! This refers to the pattern left on the snow by the grooming machines.

Cruiser:
A well-groomed slope with wide-open space for high speed, large radius turns.

Downloading:
Riding a chairlift down the mountain instead of skiing. Downloading is often used for mountain egress early or late in the season when valley snow is nonexistent.

Expert:
A term used to describe skiers and snowboarders capable of descending Double Black Diamond terrain...and make it look easy!

Gate:
The skiing equivalent of the "velvet rope". A gate is simply a break in the fence line that is opened and closed at the discretion of the ski patrol.

Grooming Map:
A map that is posted at key locations on the mountain that shows what runs were groomed the night before.

Grooming Signs :
Signs placed at key locations on the mountain that display what runs were groomed the night before.

Intermediate:
A skier or snowboarder that is capable of turning both ways and stopping. The intermediate is now able to venture into increasingly difficult terrain but may struggle in powder.

Lightboard:
A billboard which, through the illumination of specific lights, indicates which lifts are opened, closed and on standby. It may also detail how long the lines are at each lift. Lightboards are placed conveniently on both mountains.

Mogul:
A hardened lump of snow created by constant traffic over a slope that elicits dread or joy depending on the state of your knees and back.

Piste Markers:
High-visibility plastic discs on poles primarily used to mark the easiest route down from the alpine.

Powder:
Often referred to as "White Gold", powder is snow with a very low specific gravity and a tendency to make people sick for work.

Skier's Left:
The left-hand side of the ski run from the perspective of a skier sliding down the fall line.

Skier's Right:
The right-hand side of the slope from the perspective of a skier sliding down the fall line.

Snowcat:
Large machines on metal tracks, capable of grooming runs and plowing snow.

Sweep:
A term used to describe the patrol clearing of the mountain. From top to bottom the entire mountain is skied to ensure no public are left on-hill after closing.

T-Bar:
A surface based lift. Skiers and boarders use the lift by standing in front of a T shaped bar that is connected to a cable and pulls them up the hill.

Thigh Burner:
A long run requiring stamina in the quadriceps femora muscles, the term is relative, so one persons thigh burner may be another person's warm up run.

Tree Well:
A tree well is a dangerous natural phenomenon where a hole forms around the base of a tree (see safety section).

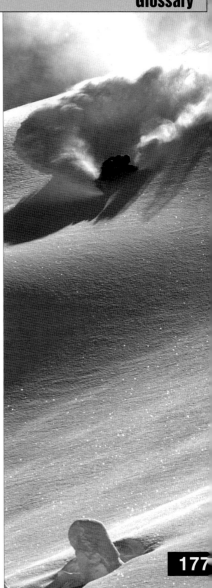

177

Index

Index

Index of Advertisers